THE INTERNATIONAL JOURNAL OF ETHICAL LEADERSHIP

Volume 8
Fall 2021

INAMORI INTERNATIONAL
CENTER FOR ETHICS
AND EXCELLENCE

The International Journal of Ethical Leadership
Case Western Reserve University
Editor-in-Chief: Shannon E. French, Inamori Professor in Ethics and
    Director, Inamori International Center for Ethics and Excellence
Executive Editor: Michael Scharf, Dean of the School of Law, John
    Deaver Drinko-Baker & Hostetler Professor of Law, and Director,
    Frederick K. Cox International Law Center
Managing Editor: Beth Trecasa, Associate Director,
    Inamori International Center for Ethics and Excellence
Copyeditor: Thea Ledendecker

The International Journal of Ethical Leadership, Volume 8, Fall 2021

All new material © 2021 *The International Journal of Ethical Leadership.*

All rights reserved • Manufactured in the United States of America

ISSN 2326-7461
ISBN: 978-1-62922-092-5

For additional information, please contact inamoricenter@case.edu
or visit case.edu/inamori

Contents

Message from the Editor

Shannon E. French
Inamori Professor in Ethics and Director,
Inamori International Center for Ethics and Excellence,
Case Western Reserve University

The global pandemic has been a terrible tragedy and a profound challenge for all of us. As well as taking far too many precious lives, this crisis has highlighted and exasperated already existing deep inequities among us. From uneven access to healthcare to an uptick in hate crimes to battles over mask wearing, social distancing, and lockdowns, we have seen humanity struggle under the strain of fear and uncertainty.

Due to the risk of COVID-19 transmission at large gatherings, we at the Inamori International Center for Ethics and Excellence and the leadership of Case Western Reserve University made the difficult decision to postpone our traditional Inamori Ethics Prize events and instead revise our overall programming for the year. Judge Silvia Fernández de Gurmendi will still be recognized with the 2020 Inamori Ethics Prize in the fall of 2021 for her outstanding ethical leadership in international justice, humanitarian law, and human rights. In the meantime, we chose to provide space to have a prolonged conversation on a topic of great consequence at this moment in history: JUSTICE. Drawing on the insight and expertise of past and present Inamori Ethics Prize winners as well as top scholars and practitioners, we hosted a thematic series of events and programming addressing the topic of justice from multiple perspectives, locally and globally: Conversations on Justice. To learn more about this series and view videos from the events, please visit our website at: case.edu/inamori. Transcripts of key events from this series are included in this volume, and they represent tremendous wisdom from diverse points of view, including:

- A general exploration of justice, as well as human and civil rights, held on October 23, 2020, with Inamori Ethics Prize winners Silvia Fernández de Gurmendi (2020), LeVar Burton (2019), Farouk El-Baz (2018), and Marian Wright Edelman (2017). This was the first time we had ever been able to bring together multiple prize winners for a conversation.

- A conversation with seventeenth Vice-Chancellor and president of the University of the South and former US Ambassador to the African Union Reuben E. Brigety II on "Overcoming American Tribalism: Healing America through Common Purpose" from February 16, 2021, which featured a robust conversation on how universities, society, and private citizens can better lead during these fractured times and develop a stronger sense of constructive civic habits.

- A panel discussion on Climate Justice held on February 26, 2021 featuring legendary environmental activist and 2012 Inamori Ethics Prize winner David Suzuki; Head of Environmental Campaigns, Grants and Activism, Patagonia, Inc., Hans Cole; Community Engagement Specialist & Diversity Coordinator, Thriving Communities, Western Reserve Land Conservancy, and Black Environmentalist Co-Founder Jacqueline Gillon; and CWRU Climate Action Network Co-Leaders Ina Martin (Operations Director, Materials for Opto/electronics Research and Education (MORE) Center) and Stephanie Corbett (Director of Energy and Sustainability and Interim Farm Director).

This volume also features articles on the theme of justice, with reflections on ethical leadership ranging from education to cyberspace. We are deeply grateful to everyone who contributed to this volume, especially in these difficult times, and we dedicate this work to everyone around the world fighting for justice and the welfare of humankind.

Thank you for taking the time to peruse these conversations and thoughts on justice.

Conversations on JUSTICE with Inamori Ethics Prize Winners
October 23, 2020

Shannon E. French
Inamori Professor in Ethics and Director of the Inamori Center for Ethics and Excellence
Silvia Alejandra Fernández de Gurmendi
leading figure in international justice, humanitarian law, and human rights, the first woman to serve as the president of the International Criminal Court (ICC), and recipient of the 2020 Inamori Ethics Prize
LeVar Burton
renowned actor-producer-writer-director, literacy and AIDS research advocate, recipient of the 2019 Inamori Ethics Prize, and first recipient honored for ethical leadership in the Arts
Farouk El-Baz
famed NASA scientist and geologist, clear water advocate, advisor to African leaders on decreasing dependence on strained water sources and finding hidden ones, and recipient of the 2018 Inamori Ethics Prize
and
Marian Wright Edelman
revered civil rights leader, the first black woman ever admitted into the Mississippi Bar, founder and president of the Children's Defense Fund, and recipient of the 2017 Inamori Ethics Prize

---

FRENCH: Welcome everyone, virtually, to the Inamori International Center for Ethics and Excellence at Case Western Reserve University in Cleveland, Ohio, USA. We're so delighted to have you with us here today for this momentous occasion where we have the opportunity to discuss justice with four of our Inamori Ethics Prize Recipients. The Inamori Ethics Prize winners were honored, each of them, for being outstanding global ethical leaders in their fields, and so we have brought the most recent four winners together today to talk about this very important, very timely, topic of justice.

3

I'm going to introduce them very briefly and myself. I am Shannon French, the director of the Center, and I'm here with our associate director, Beth Trecasa. We're going to take in the questions that you all send and make sure that they get as many as possible to our panelists, and then we will keep the conversation going until about 2:15, our time here on the East Coast. With that in mind let me very briefly introduce these wonderful individuals to you, but I would also direct you to our website for the Inamori Center for much more information on each of them and where you can also find their videos of their actual speeches that they gave when they received the award.

First our 2020 winner, who has unfortunately had to have her ceremony postponed due to the global pandemic, but she is with us here today virtually, and that is Silvia Alejandra Fernández de Gurmendi, and she is joining us all the way from Argentina. For those of you who are not familiar with her incredible history, she is a leading figure in international justice, humanitarian law, and human rights, and she was the first woman to serve as the president of the International Criminal Court, or ICC. She's worked tirelessly throughout her career to see that those who commit war crimes and crimes against humanity are held accountable for their actions. Our 2019 winner is with us here as well, and that is none other than renowned actor, producer, writer, and director, LeVar Burton. LeVar Burton, in addition to his work in the arts, has been an absolutely passionate advocate for literacy, both for children and adults, and has also worked to raise money for AIDS research. He was also our first prize winner to ever be honored for ethical leadership in the Arts. We are also joined by our 2018 recipient, Farouk El-Baz. Farouk El-Baz is a famed NASA scientist. He was the one who actually taught the Apollo astronauts what to expect when they landed on the moon and later, after he left NASA, he turned the very technology and science that he had practiced—focused towards space—and refocused it towards the Earth. Using techniques like remote sensing to look for hidden water sources in places where humans are suffering, like war-torn Darfur, and he joins us today from Boston. By the way, I didn't mention LeVar is joining us from New Orleans, which when I used to live in Texas we called N'awlins, and he will have to depart after a little while, but we're glad he could join us. Last, but certainly not least, we have another icon with us today of course, Marian Wright Edelman. She is a revered civil rights leader, the first black woman ever admitted into the Mississippi Bar. She founded the Children's Defense Fund, which is the nation's leading advocacy organization for children and families, which champions policies to lift children from poverty, protect them from abuse and neglect, and ensure their access to healthcare and quality education. These are the four amazing people that I brought together for you here today, and we're going to start by asking some questions that we already have. This is very exciting.

LeVar, I'm going to open with you if I may. LeVar, from your portrayal of Kunta Kinte in *Roots* to your work with literacy in *Reading Rainbow*, to your current podcast *LeVar Burton Reads*, and your upcoming directing of the documentary *Two-Front War*, you've advocated for the importance of sharing stories and the lived experience of Black Americans. President Trump recently issued an order to establish "patriotic education"—that's the expression he's using—to defend American history. What concerns do you have about that?

BURTON: Wow. What a great question Shannon, and first I'd just like to say I sometimes just have to pinch myself. How a storyteller wound up in the company of these world changers, I don't know, but I'm happy to just be in the same space with these people, with Silvia and Farouk and Marian. As a storyteller, here's my point of view on what Mr. Trump is suggesting. America has never told itself the true story of who we are and how we got here, and it sounds to me like Mr. Trump in addition, along with his idea of "making American great again," wants to return to a time that really never existed. The myth of American exceptionalism, in my view, is just that. It is simply a myth. The story of the founding of America is one where we came to this nation and stole the land from the people who were on it and killed anyone who resisted, and we just don't teach that to our children. We have a tendency to gloss over our history and reinvent the past in order to serve our egos. The idea of educating, creating content, and curriculum that perpetuates these myths about America is as bad an idea as I can possibly think of. However, and I will be quite honest and candid, I think this administration is full of bad ideas, and I cannot wait for it to be gone.

FRENCH: Thank you for sharing your thoughts on that, and while I've got you thinking in this vein, one of your iconic characters that so many people know you from was the engineer Geordi La Forge on *Star Trek: The Next Generation*, and as that character you were part of an optimistic view of the future. We've just talked the past and history, and *Star Trek* is that forward-looking vision. It certainly looked, to me anyway, as a more just and equitable world than the one we're currently living in, and so I'm wondering, do you still have hope that that kind of future is possible, and why or why not?

BURTON: I am always hopeful. I'm betting on the human beings. Gene Roddenberry's vision for the future was one that always appealed to me as a young black kid growing up in Sacramento, California. As a science-fiction fan, Gene's vision was one that included me, so as a storyteller he was saying, "When the future comes there is a place for you." Gene's vision for humanity was that we would indeed resolve all issues of race and class and sex and economy and live in a more egalitarian society. I still believe in our potential to get there because I believe in human beings and our ability to rise to our highest level of expression while working out all of the darker aspects of our nature. I genuinely believe, Shannon, that this current generation will get us ever closer to that ideal of living in a world that is just and equitable for all. The passion that they have shown on the streets of the world this past summer encourages me in the belief that, as Kendrick Lamar would say, "We gon' be alright."

FRENCH: I love that you have hope, and I have to say hearing that gives me more hope, so thank you very much. I have a related question that came in for Silvia, and I think it's so closely related that Silvia, I'd like to throw this one to you, if I may. In trying war criminals you've obviously had to confront some of the worst that humans are capable of doing to one another. Do you still have hope that humans, despite our differences, can learn to treat each other justly and fairly, with dignity and respect?

FERNÁNDEZ DE GURMENDI: Let me say that I'm also very very hopeful, I'm also a very optimistic person. Indeed, we have seen at the court real—you see real evil. Now, are we going to learn? I have to say that I don't know if everybody will ever learn, not everybody, but I do believe that we can, and we should make it more difficult for those who do not learn. They can do so—if they do not learn how to not do harm—we need to make it more difficult for them and we need to make national societies more resilient. Now I think prevention is key. Of course I'm going to be talking about justice, and justice is very important as a prevention tool, but certainly not the only one. They are—you know we have learned about past atrocities. We know they do not happen overnight. We know that they are processes, that they require planning and preparation, that they are warning signs and common risk factors that can lead to enable the commission of violence, of crimes. Racism, xenophobia, antisemitism, and other forms of discrimination, intolerance, and exclusion are well-known precursors of violence. Now, unfortunately, we know they are on the rise. In many of the situations at the court when—when you read the context of the crimes that were committed, you can see easily that there was a disaster in the making not for months, for years, for decades. So there is a need to address these precursors of violence early on, before they explode, and you need to have standards, you need to have policies and appropriate mechanisms permanently enshrined in the national policies, and it has been mentioned here about education. Yes, education is one of the keys in prevention. Education, sorry, not "patriotic education," but education for inclusion, education to learn tolerance, to learn how to include the others. This is extremely important. We need education, we need appropriate, permanent policies and specific initiatives to address precursors of violence, and I think we can. With that we can make societies more resilient against those who do not learn. I think we have learned that no society is new, in whatever continent, so there is a lot that can and should be done in every region and every country, but I'm very hopeful that we have learned a lot to know how to address some of these.

FRENCH: I'm grateful again for your optimism, but also for those important warnings in a way about what needs to be done in order to keep things moving in the right direction, and to note when the warning signs are there, and also the sense that no country is immune, as you just said, and that we all need to be part of trying to build cultures and communities of justice. LeVar, actually a related question that came in. I'm going to just throw back to you because it follows off nicely from what Silvia was just saying. A question about representation in the arts, again, but specifically asking why—if you could put into words—why does it matter to have in a culture like the US or anywhere—why does it matter to have people be able to recognize themselves in the arts particularly?

BURTON: Wow. What a wonderful question, Shannon. Absent healthy self-images in popular culture and media, a child grows up with a very dangerous message. A message that says, "You do not matter. You are not a part of this thing called culture." The idea of representation in the media is so critical in terms of the mental health of a society because a society that is not receiving contributions from all of its component parts is a society that's not fully expressing itself. It's not expressing itself to its highest potential, so representation is critically important in order for everyone in the society to feel valued and included in our efforts.

FRENCH: Thank you so much, and with that point I think I will turn now to our expert on the rights of children in particular. Marian, if I may ask you, when we talk about these efforts, whether it's representation, or it's Silvia's point around building a more just society and making sure that people are held accountable, I'd like to ask you—Does it make sense to start addressing inequities that specifically affect children? What is the role of justice towards children in trying to make a society better?

EDELMAN: Well in our future and investing in children preventively and equitably is going to benefit everybody. It is a disgrace in the United States of America that children are among the poorest of our age groups, and it's costly, and they are the future in so many ways. I grew up in a small segregated town in South Carolina, Bennettsville, which I love dearly, but with great parents and community co-parents who've made it very clear that though we have the external world saying we're not as valuable as white children, we knew that wasn't true because we believe that God did not make two classes of children, and that every child was sacred, and that each of us had to struggle to make a difference and to give back in service to others. I'm so grateful for the community parents and co-parents and my own parents that taught us that if you don't like the way the world is, you change it, so I've been a rebel since I was a few years old. I would wander in and switch the black and white water fountain signs that said black and white. I would—I just—I loved growing up protesting, from the time I was four or five, but I think we need to change the perception that God made two classes of children. I'm a person of faith and our church, my father and my grandfather, Baptist preachers, all made it clear that God did not make two classes of children, that every child was sacred, and that each of us had entitlement from God to realize our full-fledged potential. I've been driven by that message of my faith. The message of the examples of my family and co-parents in one community, and I love the fact that they thought the service was about each of our space for living. You see a problem you don't just say, "Why doesn't somebody something?" Here. Why don't you do something? I always felt valued as a child and always felt that I would be empowered to change the world if I didn't like the way it was.

FRENCH: I love that and the idea that we can all change everything around us, even if it's in small parts. I love the expression that never let the idea that you can't do enough stop you from doing something. We have to keep, keep moving forward. You know I want to turn now to Farouk, if I may. I was—it was occurring to me that as someone who came to America from Egypt as an immigrant and then was pulled into doing this exciting, really cutting-edge science at NASA and yet, at the same time, you were aware of the tremendous inequities that were going on in that organization. Although you've said you've even become aware of more of them as time went on, like you didn't know everything until the story of *Hidden Figures* came out, for example, but as an Egyptian immigrant, you were able to play that key role. How do you see the struggle going forward evolving to increase diversity and speak perhaps particularly to STEM fields?

EL–BAZ: I think it's so important that we—I think it's very important that we consider the fact that we are all human beings and the opportunities, as Marian just said, the opportunities should be available to all, and the people that do better can certainly be better respected and better promoted and so on. In every field, there is no question about the fact that we need more brains for better humanity in the future. We need better brains for the economic success in the future. There is no question about the fact that we need all of our intellect and our intelligence and our knowledge and our institutional—our intuitive activities to take humanity to where we think we should go, so we cannot work only on one part of our mind or our intellect. We should work on all our intellect and ability to succeed and produce human efforts that are capable to make everybody feel happy and live a beautiful life.

FRENCH: You know I love the reminder that for the size of the problems that we face as humans right now, as all of humanity, as the human race, we really can't afford to not get everyone working on them. The idea of diversity here as a strength because we need every smart person, we need every genius, we need every talent, we need every bit of creativity, we need all of that, and we're not gonna find those people if we're forcing some of them to be pushed in a corner and not have a voice, so the best of us would otherwise be hidden if we don't include them. I was thinking, too, Farouk, that one of the things that you've done, as I mentioned in your introduction—is you've asked how we can turn science towards helping the present-day problems of the world. I think that's a very hopeful move as well, and I think it makes us—it reminds us that there is something to work towards if we do all work together, if we work on the level of the kind of passion we saw in getting humans to the moon. I'm wondering, so with your work about finding untapped water sources in Darfur, where the lack of fresh water was actually a root of conflict and death in that region, do you see overall an important role for scientists in addressing injustices that do arise from practical problems?

EL-BAZ: Absolutely, there is no question about that indeed. We went to the moon based on the interpretation of satellite images of the moon, and we selected sites for the astronauts to land based on our ability to interpret photographs of the moon before they went, and we planned their excursions on the lunar surface and where to go and what kinds of materials to pick. All of that was done interpreting photographs, so as soon as the program ended we thought, "Okay, we need to look at the Earth and figure out exactly the same kind of thing. Let's look at space photographs and figure out what is it that we need to—we can learn—and what is it that we need to learn?" We did that, and the first thing that we found out was the fact that the deserts of the world are beautifully exposed, not much cloud, and therefore we can photograph them any time and we can photograph them with all kinds of equipment, including radar, and we—when we used radar, actually the radar waves penetrated through the sand and gave us a view of the solid rock layer beneath the sand. For the first time, we were able to see the surface of the desert before the sand covered it up, and that actually told us a great deal, including about the way the water used to move around these places before they dried up and the sand took over. We found out that, my God, if water was here maybe there is leftover, some of that water might be left over in the layers beneath. We tried in Egypt, and indeed there was a great deal of water beneath the channels of former rivers and where the former rivers used to lead to and my God—there was a great deal of water, and today there are thousands of acres of land being planted constantly and regularly in this location in southern Egypt based on the images of radar, so we began to say "My God, we can do this same thing everywhere else where it's in—where it is badly needed."

That immediately showed the problem of radar ability in Darfur because Darfur was a situation where the government and the local people were fighting over land and the use of water resources. We thought, "My God, let's look at the land in northwest Sudan and see what can we see," and indeed we saw an ancient lake, much like the case in Egypt, and lots of rivers that led to it, so I started talking about that. The United Nations heard about it, Ban Ki-moon, the Secretary General of the United Nations, heard about it and called me in. I explained it to him, and he said, "Maybe you can go and explain this to the locals." They said great, and he actually assigned a helicopter for me, from the UN for me. I went to Sudan, and the first thing that I did was go to the president of Sudan, who was kind of a religious nut, he was a member of the Muslim Brotherhood. So I sat with him, and the minute we started talking,

I started talking about what water meant in Islam. I told him, in the Quran, that from water we invented or presented all kinds of things, all living things came originally from water, and God did that. So he said yes, and therefore nobody should hold water from anybody else, otherwise it would be non-Islamic, nonreligious to hold water over anybody. He said yeah, so I thought that I'm going to take a—give a lecture at the university this afternoon and he said, "No, don't give it at the university, you do it right here at the Ministry of Foreign Interior. I will come. I have somebody from Germany coming, but I want to come and listen anyway." It really happened, and I went to Darfur and talked to the people and told them where is more potential for water, and it worked out very nicely based solely on the fact that we applied knowledge from science to these kinds of problems. The most important thing, as far as I'm concerned, with the whole story is the fact that I lectured a lot, just being at BU I lectured in Boston a lot, at Harvard, MIT, and Boston University many times. The BU students started an organization, a student organization, they called it "Wells for Darfur," so they collected money, a dollar at a time. One would drop a dollar at a time for a well in Darfur, and they collected over two and a half years, consistently working at it, and they collected ten thousand dollars, meaning ten thousand students participated in the collection of one dollar to make a well in Darfur. That, to me, was the most beautiful illustration of the whole spirit, of the human spirit, of that thing.

FRENCH: I love the fact that you were able to change minds by just coming at them from where they were, you know saying, " Here's what you believe, and I will show you how what we're trying to do fits with you, what you believe." Marian, if I could draw you in on that point as well. Hearing Farouk describe that persuasion that he had to go through and bringing people around to the notion that this is something that is in everyone's interest, and you must have done so much of that in your work to try to get things changed. Marian, can you tell us anything about your efforts to try to change minds, open minds, get people how—what are some tricks or stratagems that you found actually work to get people to care about the welfare of someone who isn't exactly like them?

EDELMAN: Well, growing up with Baptist parents and a mother who ran the community and was a church organist and the church fundraiser, and the father who's a Baptist minister, and I'm grateful for my childhood because I grew up with people who believed in children, who believed in faith and believed that God did not make two classes of children, and who always made it clear from the youngest times that we were sacred and were equal to any other human being and that we, those of us who had gifts, were obligated to give back to the community in service, which is the rent we each pay for living. I feel privileged to be born where I was with who I was with the community and community of parents that I had, and one of the basic things is that services are rent to pay for living, but second, if you don't like the way the world is, you go out and you figure out a way to change it. You try to do it nonviolently, but you don't complain, you see what you can do to make it better. I had those wonderful role models and examples as I grew up, so I do what my parents did, I do what my community co-parents did. When I went to historically black college and I had Dr. King and Dr. Benjamin Mays, his model and mentor and all of our mentor, that message was reinforced that we each and to make a difference, don't complain, act, serve, make the world better, don't—it's just that's what we were put on this Earth for, just to leave it better than we found it. The fact that we have millions of children who are poor is a disgrace in the richest nation on Earth. Almost 12.3 million children who are poor and many of them living in extreme poverties. It's a disgrace. It's costly. We'd rather imprison them. What kind of values is that? Rather than give them food and give them decent housing and give them a decent education and cost-effective early childhood education. That's insane. We've made some progress, and we're trying to talk about preventive investment and putting into place a more high-quality childcare system. Still have a long way to go. Preschool education, we've made great strides in giving children healthcare, but it's hard to get all these things done when it should be just a given in a nation that says it wants to provide an equal opportunity for everybody. I think that the fact that we let our children still be the poorest group of Americans, and it hurts us all, it flies in the face of what we profess to be. I think that the key goals of our nation, to the goals of children's benefit, is to end child poverty, and you can't help children without helping their parents make sure that every child gets a high-quality early childhood education, that every child gets healthcare, that every child is safe after school, and every child gets an equal education to succeed and contribute and give back, because God did not make two classes of children. I think we've been plugging along, and there are many laws in the books, but we've got to enforce them and hold on to them when people try to cut the budget. This country's weakest point is its failure to invest in its young and to live up to its values and making sure that every child feels valued and has healthcare and has a fair chance to get a good education, to give back to this country, and I think that is our Achilles heel.

FRENCH: I appreciate that so much because as someone with a young daughter at home, thinking about what world she's going into and thinking about all of her peers, and sometimes it is hard to keep that hope, foremost about the future, but if there is to be any, it is going to come from the way that we take care of our children and lift them up and move them towards a brighter tomorrow. I'm sorry, Farouk, our guest LeVar is going to have to step away; I wanted to give him a chance to say final commentary on anything with what we've been discussing here today about the importance of justice in this world.

BURTON: My final thought is this. In a world where competition has become the norm, in fact it is the way we communicate with one another more than any other modality, we communicate through our competitive nature. I think going forward, if we are going to be successful at really realizing our most full potential as a species of human beings, we need to focus our energy and attention on cooperation more than competition. The kind of just society that can come out of a society that cooperates more than it competes bodes very well, I think, for our ability to really get the job done here on Earth as we do in the heavens, as is evidenced by the work of the geniuses like Farouk.

FRENCH: Thank you so much LeVar, and good luck with your upcoming projects, and we will all anticipate them and keep up with your contributions to the arts. Thank you so much.

BURTON: It's a blessing, Shannon, and to everybody in the office, in the audience. Have a great day and a wonderful weekend.

FRENCH: Thank you so much. Bye. Farouk, you had some thoughts to jump in on following on the previous comments from Marian.

EL-BAZ: I just wanted Marian to know something that her words affected. At the time she started the Children Defense Fund, I think it was in the '70s, early '70s or something like that, and that was the time when I had just left NASA and joined the Smithsonian Institution. There was the National Air and Space Museum, and I was directing a Center for Research there, and then I was responsible for some of the exhibits, and one of the exhibits that I was personally responsible for was a place to touch the moon. We'd have to go to my buddies at NASA to convince them that we can take a piece of the moon rock and actually put it in the museum and for people to touch it, and I succeeded after a year and a half or something, and then we started designing that to be in the first hall where you center the museum so everybody can see it. At the time Michael Collins, Apollo 11 astronaut, was the head of the National Air and Space Museum, and he and I went down to the guys fixing up the exhibits to see it before its final formation. We went down and we—at the time I had heard about her work and about the Children's Fund and she was on my mind all the time for a few days because I had four daughters myself, at that time, and then when we went down to the exhibit, the design of the exhibit, I found out there was a column, a long column, like this [*gestures vertically*], and there is a place where people can put their finger on to actually touch the moon rock, so the exhibit was called "Touch the Moon." I saw it, and it's at a very high level, and then I said, "How about the children? You can't do that! You have to put that way two feet down, further below, because the kids are the ones that will be more affected than adults by touching the moon. So no, no, no, has to be lower." Michael Collins agreed with me and went down so anybody who will go to the moon, if you want to touch the moon, you have to bend a little to touch it because the children will touch it.

FRENCH: Yay, I love that! Marian, did you know about that?

EDELMAN: No, that's wonderful!

FRENCH: What a wonderful connection between our perspectives. I love when those come up. I also thought it was cute that *Star Trek: The Next Generation*, that LeVar starred on, had a space shuttle that was named *Farouk*, it was "The El-Baz," so these worlds colliding.

EL-BAZ: I have something for LeVar, I'm sorry that he left, but I will say it, and then you can tell him about it.

FRENCH: Wonderful. Well, what I wanted to bring out—I also have a question that relates to Silvia and your work internationally. Folks who are coming in are asking about various aspects of justice, and while they clearly want to be optimistic, there's some concerns being raised about different concepts of justice around the world, but the work you've done for the International Criminal Court does depend on the idea that right and wrong are not entirely, culturally dependent, that some things really are crimes against all of humanity. Wherever they occur. Whenever they occur. Have you seen progress in your lifetime of people around the world accepting the concept of universal human rights like that?

FERNÁNDEZ DE GURMENDI: Well, I have to say yes, what I have seen in my lifetime is a meteoric rise, since the last decade of the twentieth century, of the acceptance of the concept of justice for certain category of crimes or for certain category of atrocities, mainly genocide, crimes against humanity, and war crimes. And not just divine justice or moral justice or different types of justice. Very concrete criminal justice for the perpetrators of the worst crimes, and I was privileged to see the rights, and I was also privileged to see this in functioning. Actually I cannot say now, but I remember the first case that we had at the International Criminal Court was a case for crimes committed against children, not child soldiers recruiting forcibly, children to be used in hostilities. This was a major breakthrough in the '90s, it was like a dream. It was fifty years after the Nuremberg Tribunals that we all studied in school, in the second World War, and then there were five decades where nothing like that could be accomplished again. Then in the '90s, for various reasons that we will not discuss now, you see that there was this acceptance first as a recognition of certain standards or prohibitions, again the prohibition of certain category of crimes that I have mentioned, and then most importantly, the acceptance that these types of crimes are an affront to mankind as a whole, and that you cannot leave the response to national states, but that you do also need an international response when there is no national response.

I was privileged to see these achievements that included the creation of an International Criminal Court. And you said, "Well are these universal? How universal are they, these standards and these concepts? Most importantly, are we going—are they going to survive our lifetime?" Well I have to say that the court and the recognition of these standards was created in a process that was open-ended to all states in the world, all regions of the world, and through multilateral diplomacy they came to this treaty—[*bad connection*]—with global participation in it yet only two thirds, I say only but it's quite significant, two thirds of the world is there, but most importantly even now where we are seeing a fractured world where certain pushback against internationalism—[*bad connection*]—towards national principles of noninterference going back to your frontiers, we can still see that this request for justice is still there, and it is really, there is a huge demand for justice for these types of crimes. First of all, no one really is questioning the prohibitions. No one is saying that the genocide or crimes against humanity is a legitimate response to conflict. They may try to hide the facts, they might try to deny them, put them under the rack, deny responsibility for them, but they are not denying the concept. There you have common values, and then well the ICC, the International Criminal Court, is now under attack, not everywhere, but you see a proliferation of proceedings for these type of crimes in other tribunals at the national level where there is no agreement in who is going to be prosecuting. You create mechanisms to safeguard the evidence for the future. This is happening. They created two international mechanisms for Myanmar and Syria to safeguard the evidence that is being collected, and many times collected due to science and science to digital technology, so this is being collected for future prosecutions, and actually next week there are some proceedings that are resuming in Germany, in Koblenz, against two of the Syrian officers in national proceedings for international crimes, so I'm very optimistic that even in the current environment that is very difficult and very different from the '90s, I still see that there is a lot going on and that there are indeed certain common values that remain, and I think they're here to stay.

FRENCH: I am glad to hear that, and I like hearing the history and seeing the changes and again the ways that you had to persuade or bring people along, but your point is also extremely well made that it wasn't that hard to get people to agree that certain things are wrong. People may try to get away with not calling something for example, in the case you gave calling—not calling something genocide and so forth, but you're at least able to say there isn't anyone saying, "Oh genocide is fine," so you know this is moral progress because certainly we can go further back in history where there would have been people saying that is fine, so let us see that as a move of the needle in the right direction and going towards. One of the—speaking of children, who keep coming up in our conversation, one of our younger audience members from Shaker Heights High School nearby us actually wanted a follow-up question to you, Silvia, wondering if having seen the progress that you've seen in that area, in criminal prosecutions of war criminals, do you also, just personally, think that we could see in our lifetimes ethical agreements internationally around other issues like environment, economy, and health? These kids have easy questions, obviously.

FERNÁNDEZ DE GURMENDI: This is an extremely relevant question and extremely important. I think you have all seen that I'm part of the optimistic type of individuals, so I do think that we can and should reach agreements in these areas as well. Actually, we have some agreements in issues of environment, and on other issues we really need to tackle inequality because this, together with conflict, together with climate change, is creating a crisis of huge proportions. I do think that we can do this, but of course, it requires, and I think some—I think LeVar mentioned this already, we need a lot of cooperation. We need a coordinated approach. We need multilateralism, multilateral institutions, international institutions where we can discuss, reflect, and have agreements. It's not going to be easy because, as I said, we are in a world with that you have different tendencies, and right now you have this tendency that countries think that in order to save yourself from global responses then you go back to your frontiers. I think we need to do opposite; I think we need to cooperate. This needs a huge amount of cooperation between not only states, I think we can all help. It is a dialogue and an engagement that needs to—you need to have all actors included, you need to have states, you have to have civil society, academia, students, or you know. Look at the students, look at the young people. They are all pushing out for the importance to protect their environment. There you see that you don't need only adults or superpowers. Children, students, young students are doing a huge amount to promote these agreements. Yes, with this type of young people and these activities, of course I'm very optimistic that we can do better than we are doing now.

FRENCH: Thank you so much, and another question came in for Farouk relating to your story, which people seem to be loving, about making sure the children could touch the moon. I do love that as an image, and they wanted to ask you if you have suggestions for making sure that people can think beyond the present moment? I think what they're getting at is that things like a journey to the moon or any of those projects are often very long in scale and time scale, and it can be hard to get people excited to take on something that may take years and years to come to fruition, and they were wondering if you could talk about how do you help people as a teacher, as a mentor, to maintain that kind excitement so that they're always reaching for the moon, as it were?

EL-BAZ: Indeed, it's an excellent question and indeed, it might be—it might look as if it is difficult or long-term, and maybe we should not start it now because we will not end it, but that is not at all the situation. I really think that people have thought about flying, and they did it, and in less than one hundred years we've been with you to the moon, in less than one hundred years from learning how to fly. That there is—all kinds of things that develop swiftly, even though it looks as if it is, not now or not in the near future, but indeed, it's okay. Think about it now, think about what to do, because during the 1960s we had the Apollo astronauts. They were all military guys and the guys, because there were no military women at the time and these—in the Air Force and the Navy and so on, they were all men. Now there are all kinds of women flying into space and younger people and people that were not part of the flying scheme, and in the future there will be others, and there will be many more varieties of people flying and going to Mars or going to other planetary bodies. There is no question about the fact that the more we dream, the more we expect things to happen, the more we will get there. Don't think that this is since it's one hundred years off today that it might be so difficult, and let's not do it. Absolutely not. Think about it now, and think that you are going to do it, girl or boy, that doesn't matter. You are going to do it and you are going to do well, and you're going to do something nobody else has done. Why not? It will happen. I think you need to think positive and do whatever you can. Dream as much as you can, and continue to dream because you will get there, no question about it.

FRENCH: Thank you so much, and I noticed that our questions are converging in interesting ways that we're getting in from folks. This one is directed at Marian, but it's a wonderful follow-up on what Farouk just said. Marian, and I like the language here, someone would like to know, How do you motivate yourself to keep going when some fights seem never-ending, and you feel small?

EDELMAN: You never let yourself feel small. You're never too small to make a difference, you can always make a difference. My parents in my small, segregated town made it very clear that they believed that every child was sacred and, even though it was a segregated world, that we could change it. Well I was a rebel, from the time I was four when I would switch the white and black water signs on the public department stores, but I think that we can make a difference and we've seen extraordinary change, but God did not make two classes of children. All great faiths affirm the sacredness of children, and I think we should just hold that in mind. Secondly, if you see a problem, don't just say, "Why doesn't somebody do something?" What can you do? I think each of us can do that, and I think that we've been able to see an awful lot of people come together over the last decade since Children's Defense Fund began to pass many laws that have helped millions of children escape poverty. Millions of children, they have healthcare. Millions of children get better chances to succeed in life because of a better child welfare system. Millions of children got in childcare. You do what needs to be done. Don't let anybody tell you can't change things, and that change is hard, but you got to keep at it. You're going to have to take two steps backwards, but you just have to keep moving forward. I'm really very pleased that there are many laws on the books now that have given many, many millions of children, tens of millions of children, healthcare and mental healthcare, a chance to go and get preschool education, to get a head start, to get better quality child care, but we've got much more to do. This is a very rich nation, but still twelve and a half million children live in poverty. It's disgraceful, it's costly, and we must change it, but we just must absolutely never give up advocating for preventive investment, saving money by investing in children who will become productive citizens, rather than prisons, but we're more willing to pay three times more for prisoners than for public school kids, and that's something wrong with the values of the system. I think that children deserve to have first place at the table of hope and of the future, and they are the future, and I think that while I'm proud that many, many laws are in the books, I am not proud still at the wild distribution of wealth between those at the top, and the top one and two percent, and the millions of those who are still suffering and languishing without adequate housing and adequate food and adequate hope and adequate education, that each of us feel more privileged and want for our own children. I think that the mistreatment, the failure to invest in all of our children, to live up to our values, that everybody is equal, and we should have a chance to achieve a level of equality in our society, is going to be our undoing and we are still more willing to pay three times more for prison than for public school. People, there's something really wrong with that, and I think that, you know, we must end child poverty. We must make sure that every child gets what each parent wants with their own children: decent healthcare, safety, decent place to live, housing, disability. And that should be a "duh" in this wealthy, boastfully wealthy, nation. We can continue to send people off to prison, we can continue to let millions grow up without the education they need to give back to the rest of us, but it's a spiritual poverty that must be addressed, it's a practical poverty that must be addressed. What is it about us that is more willing to put three times more to send a child off to juvenile penitention or to adult prison than to give them a good preschool education and give them healthcare, the basic things that each parent wants for their own child—

FRENCH: I'm so sorry to interrupt, I just got excited. I just wanted to jump in on—I was just moved by your point around the money that's going in the wrong direction. The money that's going to prisons and so forth, and I just wanted to push, I agree with you that it seems like it should be a "duh," that this is not right, but I'm just going to ask it straight out. Why isn't it? Who, what is the pushback? Is it—what do people think? Why are they putting the money in the wrong place? Is it that they fundamentally misunderstand what is best for children, or is there something financial behind it, that they're trying to make money? What do you think it is really? Because otherwise it just seems like insanity—

EDELMAN: We have a great pandemic here in this country. For those who are at the top and the few, we need a concept of enough. I wouldn't deprive anybody of their first million or two million or ten million or two billion, if we had no hungry children, okay? If we had no uneducated children, if we had no children that didn't get an early education that those of us were more privileged can get. This whole concept of "enough" and wanting for your own children what you want for other people's children, and that's the only way we're going to all have a safe environment in order to grow up. It defies any sense of core values and about respect for all human beings that we will let twelve and a half million children go in poverty. We're a little more willing to pay three times more to put them in prison than give them a good preschool education. What is it about us in America? We need to come to grips with our spiritual poverty. We need to come together about practical poverty. I mean but there's nobody super, but we're more willing to wait until somebody gets into trouble, and two, three times more often you imprison them than if you give them a preschool education. What is our value gap here that we need to address in the faith community, and how do we get to live up to all these things of life and liberty and justice for everybody? We need to stop this hypocrisy.

FRENCH: Farouk, I'm going to put you on the spot, too because we're talking about, what we certainly want to talk about the hope and the optimism, and I think that's vital because we all, all of us, need to keep working, and we need that spirit to do so, but I do think that we have to also ask what's gone wrong? What is going the wrong direction, and I wonder if you could talk at all from your experience, Farouk, if you see some of these same strange choices, and whether that's specifically in your work or just in society, but where it doesn't make sense to you that the direction the money is flowing? Like, why aren't we finding water for people who need it? Why aren't we? Do you have any thoughts around that?

EL-BAZ: To me, there is an objection to "the other." The ones that look different, the ones that speak different, and the ones that behave differently in any way, or dress differently or whatever, so the fear of "the other" can hold human beings further away, like the ones that have the money, the ones that have the cars and this and that, cannot perceive what is the person that walks all the time, and this and that and doesn't even have money to go into a bus or something like that. There is a vast difference between these two, and the rich and the well-to-do stay away from it all. They don't really like to see these people that don't have it, and there is an objection to their state, but there is a rejection of them. That's why we have kind of a standoffish attitude because the people that have it don't really like to consider the ones that don't have it and their problems and their life. The only thing that can get us all together is that the spiritual effect that people speak about, like Marian speaks about her church, that keeps it this and that yes, indeed the churches can do this. They, the religious people, can do that. The ones that have the potential of speaking anywhere. Writers, the movies, the television—all of these things can improve the situation a little bit by getting two parties to a little better, a little closer, a little more understanding of each other.

FRENCH: Thank you, and I think the work that LeVar was describing fits into that as well. The idea that as long as we don't have enough representations of different kinds of people then again, we won't be treating everyone the same or making people feel like they're part of the same endeavor. That cooperation that we all keep talking about won't be there. Silvia I feel—I'm gonna continue—this is a somewhat negative thread, but I do think it's important that we be addressing it. You mentioned earlier that the ICC has been under some attack, and that's certainly the case, that there has been fierce criticism, and particularly from the United States towards the International Criminal Court, and I wonder if you could say for us your thoughts on why you think there's an uptick in that? Where is that hostility coming from, and what's driving it, and any thoughts you have around why that's happening right now?

FERNÁNDEZ DE GURMENDI: Well, creating a court of the general character like the ICC was considered to be a revolution—[*bad connection*]—to be restrained, refrained by the rule of law and to accept that someone else is going to step in if you don't do what is necessary to address certain facts. So already to have states accepting this was a huge thing, and the second huge matter is that in accepting this international response, the international community accepted also to create a court where the court itself can decide where to look and where to step in. So it is not a surprise that this court was not created by superpowers, it was not created by huge powerful countries. They were created by those who most need the law, which is midsize and small countries; in a way the law is an equalizer, but that is not easy to accept for those who do not need the protection of the law. Every time the court has selected a situation to investigate and prosecute, that has created a lot of problems because as I said there is a general recognition of standards, but there is more difficult acceptance of having this address to you or to your friends, so that has created problems, every time the court has selected a situation it has created huge problems, and one of the situations that was starting to be investigated by the court was Darfur. Farouk was talking about Darfur and the conflicts of water, and this was a situation where everybody agreed that there were huge atrocities being committed there, and the situation was brought by the court, actually by the Security Council of the United Nations, and you would think that everybody would accept this, and at the time Sudan didn't accept it; of course now they do because they have changed, but every situation, even the most obvious ones for people, create a lot of problems. The court has moved from situations in Africa and that was criticized because they were saying, "Well the court is focusing too much on Africa, why don't they go elsewhere?" The court also started to investigate in other regions of the world, in Georgia, in Afghanistan, where other countries have also an interest, and they are following these situations. That was not very well received by other states, and it was not received, as you mentioned, by the United States, so there is an issue there of maybe protecting self-interest, and also there is another issue, which I always said and I always said it when I was at the court, that the court has some problems with its own performance. It was too slow, it was considered not to be sufficiently efficient, so there has been a big push to reform, to accelerate proceedings, to expedite, to make the selection of situations more transparent. That is being done. Actually they are under this process of reform right now, and it has started already, and I did my small contribution to this in the past. We need to improve the quality of justice that is delivered in order to obtain more cooperation, but we also have to accept that when you go into global, general standards, sometimes you are affecting interest of specific countries and specific regions, and the court will need to live with this, and I hope that it will be receiving sufficient protection and cooperation from other regions of the world as well because that is what will allow it to survive.

FRENCH: Thank you. I appreciate again the history is helpful and also the specific examples and again connecting up to Farouk's work with Darfur, but showing how these struggles are ongoing, this is the current state of what we are trying to achieve, and it brought out another question, Marian, that someone brought in based on what Silvia was describing with the International Criminal Court. What was asking about—for Marian to comment on specifically systemic racism, institutional racism in the United States, and how it has come into things like police behavior and the court system, and how you see changes that need to be made in that particular area to combat that problem? How do you see justice as almost an institution? It looks like the question is around justice as an institution, whether that's the law side or the order side, how does that need to confront systemic racism going forward?

EDELMAN: It has to. We have an unjust criminal justice system in so many ways. I'm just very pleased with what young people have been doing and Black Lives Matter and calling into question the way in which law enforcement treats disproportionately people of color differently and then unfairly than people who are not of color. We have, we in the United States, we have a legacy of slavery that has never really gone away and been eradicated, and we've made strides forward and different movements before the Civil War. We had a reconstruction period, another post-reconstruction period. Change is never permanent. We're back in another period of demand for equal access to justice and to the richness of this nation for all of us, but we've got a long way to go. When we look at the prison population, it's disproportionately poorer minorities. When we look at unequal education, it is still too much true for many of our children of color in our inner cities, in rural areas. We still have structural problems that come from our legacy of slavery and from segregation and from apartheid. When we look at the income, the distribution of income in this country would be the Forbes 100, yeah they're great, they may look great as what the top one percent is, one tenth of one percent yet, we have twelve and a half million children living in poverty. There's something wrong and unjust in that picture. We've got to create a concept of "enough." I don't begrudge their first, their second, or ten, or fifteen million or even their billion or their second billion, if we have not got twelve and a half million poor children, many of them living in extreme poverty, if we do not have children who don't still get adequate healthcare, or who are being put out in the child welfare system without adequate chances to grow up into a successful adulthood. There's something wrong with twelve and a half million poor children, many millions of them in extreme poverty, in an economy like the United States of America. We need to come to come to grips and just to make sure there's a concept of "enough for all" and that every child has a fair chance to get educated, to have healthcare, to be able to realize their God-given potential, and that still does not exist in the United States of America, and we must correct it. There should be no poor children in the United States of America. We can't afford not to do it. There should not be billionaires and billionaires with trillions when we've got twelve and a half million poor children. Something is wrong in that system. We need to change it.

FRENCH: Thank you, and I think the person who asked the question will appreciate that you went into some depth on the point that this is not really and should not be seen as completely unsolvable. There are solutions, we're aware of some of the solutions, but what we need is the will. I think that's a really important point to bring in there, that this is not like some of the mysteries of the world where we really haven't figured it out yet. We know how we could solve some of these, but we need the political will behind it. Farouk, I'm going to blend a few questions because they're directed at you, around the fact that you are an educator, that you've been an educator your whole life. Someone references having seen the episode of *From the Earth to the Moon* where you were portrayed as educating the Apollo scientists, but their question is—they're wondering, I'm guessing they're an educator too, I don't know at what level—but they're asking, Do you think there are helpful ways to think about and incorporate some of the topics we've talked about here today as an educator in whatever you're teaching, for example, so that you don't have to be specifically teaching a course on justice to bring up some of these points, or do you think that doesn't make sense, and you should just stick to science if you're doing science and not touch on any social issues? That was the question around, or I'm blending a couple, but they want to know about learning about justice and blending into your process as an educator.

EL-BAZ: There is no question in my mind at all that as you educate, you can blend in all kinds of things with it because you don't need to educate something about science and skip everything else about the fact that—What does science do? Science helps people. Well, helps people do what? Well, better lives. Better lives, meaning where? I know all of that, it really is if you can educate, you can educate in all kinds of fields and really blend them together, and if you are a good teacher then you can look at the environment of the students themselves. See where they came from. What is the problem when they leave school? Where they go to go home, what is that place where they live in, and how can you discuss things in a way for them to take it better, to appreciate it a bit more, and to ask more questions, to actually revel, to enjoy being taught? Good teachers are like that, they can see what their students are and see what they ask about, and they can sense what they are after, and they respond with them. They give them the basic stuff that they have to teach in a way that they, the students, can absorb it, they can appreciate it, can simmer, have it in their thoughts and delight them while they are learning, and make them happy while they are learning. The answer is absolutely, yes, you can blend these things together.

FRENCH: I like that, and it makes me want to take a class from you. I think that would be marvelous. Silvia, we have another question that's come in for you around the issue of deterrents, and the question has to do with the fact that so much work happens after crimes have been committed, obviously, in terms of things like the sorts of crimes that end up before the ICC. Do you have any thoughts about how the international community can do more around deterrence, and I think you mentioned some of this in one of your earlier answers, but they were intrigued and would like to hear more on your thoughts of what might work for building a more just world when it comes to deterrence?

FERNÁNDEZ DE GURMENDI: Well first of all, justice is supposed to act as a deterrent. When you talk about deterrence, deterrence means a little bit of a threat, in a way. You say, "Well if you do this you will end up in front of justice." That of course, it's a very narrow understanding of prevention, but it is an aspect of it. One problem with that deterrent effect of justice and all these tribunals have been created on the understanding that justice can prevent future crimes actually. If you go into the wrong treaty, the wrong statutes that created the court, it says that. We do—that we have seen a lot of atrocities, and with this we hope to prevent future crimes. Now, one problem that we have there is, again, the fact that justice, even if it is a far wider demand for justice and much more is being done than it was done, I would say three decades ago nothing was done. I would say that we come—the entire twentieth century, from Nuremberg to the end, was basically an age of impunity. It was easier to go to prison if you stole a car than if you committed genocide because normally, if you committed genocide there will be a solution, there will be an agreement, there will be impunity, and then you will go to some villa in the south of some country to relax until the end of your life. We have gone from that to justice efforts, but it is still very little. There is no pattern of accountability. We need, first of all we need more justice; we need really more proceedings, more ratifications of the ICC, less attacks from the ICC, and more justice in general, nationally and internationally. But that is one aspect you need to do a lot around, and it has been said here, you need to invest in prevention, you have to invest in inequality, you have to invest in things that make a lot of sense. Now the problem is that I think most politicians, in every country, will go for short-term approaches to things. You say you need to invest in education in order to teach more about inclusion, nondiscrimination, nonracism, but those are long-term efforts, so most politicians want short-term efforts, not long-term efforts, but actually that's what we need because it makes a lot of sense. Marian was mentioning about a spirituality gap or a value gap; well we do have that, of course, but we also have a lack of understanding in self-interest because it is in self-interest to invest in early warnings against violence, to invest in health, to invest in education, to invest in initiatives against discrimination. Again, what we need to do is to push our governments, to push our politicians to invest in these long-term projects that will diminish the sources of violence. The justice comes because you have not addressed the sources. Of course you can help that, that will prevent the future, but actually if you need to go and do justice against the perpetrator of genocide you can say, well already you have failed, because you failed to prevent what should have never happened. So what would work? Again, there is no simple magic solution. There is a concerted effort and coordinated efforts of all of us, including at the national level, to push our governments to do the right thing. Don't let them go away without investing in what is right to prevent violence and improve the world.

FRENCH: Thank you, and Marian, I'm wondering if you might want to jump in here because I could see you reacting with agreement to some of the things Silvia was saying, and I am wondering about this idea. I assume from some of your work, Marian, that you have seen the literal playing out of what she was describing. That when resources are given to people in the front end, as it were, given to people preventatively, then you don't see the same kinds of problems later on, that there is actual proof of this process, is that correct?

EDELMAN: Preventative investment works. Investing in children early on to give them their basic healthcare, their basic nutrition—what we want for our own children, okay—and basic safe housing, and basic early childhood education, all these are doable, and we can still have lots of room for billionaires to be billionaires. They don't need to have a hundred billion or a trillion, but there could be a concept of "enough for all" at the bottom so that every child would have a chance to succeed and perhaps one of these days become a millionaire, billionaire if that's what they want to be. But this is not rocket science; we just have a degree of injustice in the distribution of resources and access to the resources that has to be corrected at some point. We just don't—you know I don't begrudge anybody their first, second, and third billion, if we didn't have all these poor millions of children and extremely poor children in our own rich nation and around the world. We can do better than that. We could end child poverty in our nation and still have lots of millionaires and billionaires around. You know we can do better than this. It needs to be a concept of enough for every human being. God did not make two classes of children, I don't believe, and we should not continue to do that by the way in which our systems have been designed to create those systems.

FRENCH: Thank you very much. Now the next question is technically directed to all of you because they want to hear your perspectives, each of you on this. I'm going to start with you, Farouk, if I may? The question is that each of you is renowned in your own field, and you have the opportunity, either directly or indirectly, to speak to diverse audiences around the world. They want to know, How has your public profile become part of your identity, and in what ways have you been able to use that profile as a way to enact or encourage change? And they were asking for even some specifics as well as generalized, so things like, Do you use social media? How do you get your voice out there? How do you use your profile and the status that you have earned to try to enact or encourage change in the world?

EL-BAZ: This is an excellent question because that is really the basis or the reason for being able to make change, and I definitely am open to all kinds of social media. I have accounts everywhere, and I use them all the time, and I respond particularly to youth in Arab worlds in general. I get more comments and more attention and more requests from youth, from teenagers and people in their twenties and up to their thirties, from all kinds of Arab countries everywhere constantly about their jobs, about their ideas, about latitude, about what should they do with the government, about what should they study and how could they study and what is best for them, and you name it. That is, as far as I'm concerned, the place where we can be most effective, because we speak directly to these people that we do not have anything to gain from talking one way or the other.

They know they are not paying us to do it so there is no benefit either from me or them and therefore my advice to them will be directed at basically their benefit, and there is nothing else that I can do except for that, and therefore I open myself constantly. Even now with the coronavirus I'm online constantly with the students in university in Alexandria, in Cairo, everywhere in universities and groups and people in the UAE and Saudi Arabia and Qatar, in Kuwait, everywhere where people speak Arabic, and they know of me. They communicate, and I respond, and it is a wonderful thing because I think we can certainly make a change ourselves.

FRENCH: And I have to say, your Twitter profile is excellent. I follow you on Twitter myself, so I encourage others to do the same. Marian, same question to you, and if you have any specifics? I know you have recently, if I'm correct, you have stepped down from running the Children's Defense Fund, but you obviously still have a platform and a voice. How do you get that voice out there in a variety of ways?

EDELMAN: The ways in which I've been doing the last fifty years. I try to stay out in community, I try to knock on doors and be in direct contact with the poor. Social media has its role, television has its role, but there is no substitute for knocking on doors and talking to people and sitting with people and praying with people, and I'm still for grassroots organizing, and I'm for creating models that implement change in local communities that empower people, empower young people. I'm very proud of the new generation and what I call servant leaders that are developing out of our Freedom Schools Programs. Our children who we've been celebrating, who've been beating the odds, who can show other young people that you can make it no matter what. If your dad is in prison or your mother's in prison, or you saw somebody shot, or you know you were shot, you can make it. We just need to build on the strength and the resiliency of many of those left behind and to create grassroots movements at the local level. I'm very proud of our Freedom Schools. I'm very proud of the servant leaders that are coming out of our Beat the Odds kids, who've got in prison fathers and mothers, but they have somehow—if one person reaches out to them and says, "You can make it, you know you can do this," but we've just got to forage change at the bottom that builds up. I believe my theory of change is the parable of the sower: you've got to plant a lot of seeds from the bottom up, and the sun's going to burn up a lot of those seeds and pour all kinds of stuff on a lot of those seeds, but when you plant enough of them. I've watched our seeds and the Children's Defense Fund grow and I'm so proud of our young people who have beat the odds, whose parents are in prison, but somehow they're able to get away from that as the future because there's somebody in that community who made a difference. I'm more proud of our freedom schools in many ways because they're learning that they can learn how to read and catch up. We just need to do what we've got to do at the grassroots level and to make sure that policy reflects the needs of people in their communities day to day, and I think that making sure that young people are engaged at every level, we don't have any right to give up on a child, and that we just need to build that movement, but it has to come from the bottom up and not just from the top down.

FRENCH: Thank you, and I love that we've now gotten two different perspectives, but they're not mutually exclusive, and that's wonderful as well. You can use the right there, face to face in the community when we can, the pandemic being in the way for some of that at the moment, and also, the media that can reach halfway across the world and bring someone close in a different sense. I'm going to turn the same question to you, Silvia, and again just to restate the core aspect of it, they want to know how your public profile, you know, you were the first woman president of the ICC, for example, How has your public profile become part of your identity, and how have you been able to use that profile, and in what specific ways have you tried to enact or encourage change?

FERNÁNDEZ DE GURMENDI: Well this is a great question, and actually in a way you also formulated that beginning as, "Well you have to become renowned in your own field," and I would say that is already a little bit of a problem because when you are renowned in your own field, you tend to stay in your own field and talk a lot with other people that are in the same field, so you end up talking to those who do not need you to talk, and sometimes you are talking among yourselves. What I'm trying to do a lot is to get a little bit out of this field. Of course I do talk a lot there, and I use my public profile to try to disseminate the idea of justice, but not just to others in the field, but those who are not in the field, those students, but also you try to go into areas of people doing things that may be related but not really so specific. You may have noticed that I've been speaking a lot on issues of prevention because, indeed, I'm involved very much in issues of education and issues of prevention beyond justice. For instance, I'm now a part of what is called Global Action Alliance Against Mass Atrocity which is a platform prevention, and there I'm involved with people that come from various different fields including things that are nothing related to the law or justice. I'm also part of the International Alliance for the Remembrance of Holocaust, which really goes very much into training and education in order to understand from the past how to prevent for the future. I'm really trying to get out a little bit, and I'm trying to connect the dots myself, but also help others to connect. You know, putting organizations in touch with each other, they also start enhancing their coordination and cooperation around certain areas and that achieves amazing, amazing results. In order to do that I talk a lot, I write a lot. Now that we are, I have been in the lockdown for seven months now in Argentina, so that means Zooms and virtual meetings and which in a way has helped to connect with people that I may not be able to see in a normal life before the pandemic. I'm very bad in social media. I do have a Twitter account. You will see that I have never published one tweet, but I do follow others in order to be informed. I use more traditional ways of communication, and that is also very tiring and exhausting, but I also believe very much in connecting with, well real people are not real anymore in these pandemic times, but still connecting more in a one-to-one or small circles in order to go from there to larger circles, so this is a little bit of what I do.

FRENCH: Thank you so much. Now I can't believe it, and I know there's going to be a bunch of people saying, "Ah, you didn't get to my question!" and I'm so sorry, but we—are believe it or not—almost out of time; it just shows how much passion and interest people have around this topic of justice. I would like with our very few remaining minutes just to briefly give each of you a chance to say a short final word to the folks listening. Just anything else you'd like to say about working towards justice. Farouk, let's start with you again, if we may?

EL–BAZ: It's very important that each one of us would when you see something wrong, try to do something about it or try to tell others how to do about it. The way we're gonna change is by talking to each other, there's no question about it, and learning from each other, so be a little more careful of listening to others. Watch how others behave and what they say and be kind to them and help them to understand things differently and be nice and be kind and talk to them about what could be done better. It always works. I find that it is in every case that I tried, it works.

FRENCH: I have to say again all of this is giving me hope. Marian, final thoughts from you?

EDELMAN: I have two slave women who guide me and get me up when I get lazy or I think that I can't make a difference. One of them is Sojourner Truth who has a theory of—I loved one story that she was heckled by an old white man in New Orleans who said he, "Didn't care anymore about her anti-slavery talking than he did for an old flea bite," and she snapped back at him and said "That's all right the Lord willing we'll keep you scratching." Many of us like to be big dogs; we just need to be strategic fleas. Enough fleas biting strategically and persistently can move the biggest dogs and the biggest policies, and that's been our theory of the Children's Defense Fund. Get out there with your vote, be a flea. Get out there and organize with your church women, your missionary women, your mother's clubs and others and work it up from the bottom. Be a flea. Massive flea corps of people who will bite others in power who are treating children and the poor unjustly can make a difference. We've seen a lot of laws get enacted because of that. A lot of fleas voting, nagging, showing up in the most inconvenient places to make politicians uncomfortable. A lot of laws on the books as a result of those fleas out there. You don't have to be big dogs, just make sure that you see an injustice. If you see an injustice, don't just be quiet about it, speak up, and then go grab the people in your own community and your own church and your own clubs and say, "What am I going to do about it?" Don't ask the question and expect somebody else do something about it, and so I just think that the whole point is to take responsibility for being a justice flea wherever you are and whatever your institution is. Institution of faith, in your sorority, your fraternity, in your fraternal organizations whatever, but let's just make a difference in making the world fit for the next generations of children so that we leave them something better than we found.

FRENCH: I love it and I dedicate myself to being a strategic flea, that's marvelous. Silvia, from you?

FERNÁNDEZ DE GURMENDI: I would like to pick on something that was said I think by Marian, when she said, "You're never too small to make a difference," and I would like to elaborate on that. I love that phrase, and I think I would like to elaborate to say that whatever you do is never too small to make a difference because when you're dealing with mass atrocities, when you are dealing with millions of displaced people, when you are dealing with so much suffering you wonder, and I have wondered, what difference did it make to indict a few perpetrators or to send to prison one person when you see all this. What is the point of going to investigate a crime in the north when you see all the crimes that are being committed in the south, in the east, and the west? Well it's a little bit like you say, this is just a drop in the ocean, does it make any difference? I frankly believe it does. It does make a concrete difference for concrete people, and I have seen it with my own eyes. You are not helping humanity, but you are helping part of humanity, even if it is a tiny part, and I think that makes a difference for concrete people and that I think is what we need to do. A little bit, one step at a time, but that step makes the difference. So I think it is worth pursuing even if sometimes you believe "what for?" Well, for those who really see the impact of whatever you're doing, and it makes a difference to them.

FRENCH: That's marvelous. Change one life and you change the world. I have been so inspired by all of you and by LeVar who was with us earlier. I want to thank you all so much. If we had a live audience you would hear ovation very loud and cheers because you've taken us to many important and valuable places today. I want to thank you all, and I also want to thank our campus partners, everyone who supports the Inamori Center and our work and our mission, and the wonderful audience that joined us and sent us all those great questions. I'd also like to encourage those of you who have enjoyed this conversation to please keep an eye on the Inamori Center website and look out for future events. This is part of a series of Conversations on Justice. Of course we will—we are going to believe that the pandemic is going to end, and we are going to be able to eventually bring Silvia to our campus to be properly presented with her with her Inamori Ethics Prize as well. All of those things will be upcoming as events and we'd love to bring you all back for all of those. Thank you so much, my friends. I really appreciate this, and I know that everyone listening has as well. Thank you and have a great rest of your day or evening.

Conversations on Climate JUSTICE with Inamori Ethics Prize Winner & Colleagues
February 26, 2021

Shannon E. French
Inamori Professor in Ethics and Director of the Inamori Center for Ethics and Excellence
David Suzuki
Legendary environmental activist and 2012 Inamori Ethics Prize winner
Hans Cole
Head of Environmental Campaigns, Grants and Activism, Patagonia
Jacqueline Gillon
Community Engagement Specialist & Diversity Coordinator, Thriving Communities, Western Reserve Land Conservancy and Black Environmental Leaders Co-Leader
and
CWRU Culture Change for Climate Change Co-Leaders:
Ina Martin
Operations Director, Materials for Opto/electronics Research and Education (MORE) Center
Stephanie Corbett
Director of Energy and Sustainability and Interim Farm Director

---

FRENCH: Welcome everyone, virtually at least, to the International Center for Ethics and Excellence at Case Western Reserve University in Cleveland, Ohio. My name is Shannon French, and I'm the director of the Inamori Center, and I'm joined here today by our associate director Beth Trecasa. We're delighted that you could join us in this online world to have another in our series of Conversations on Justice. Today our focus is going to be on climate justice. We truly have some amazing panelists with us here today to make sure that this is a great conversation. I'm actually going to introduce each of them extremely briefly, so I hope you will take some time and read about them on your own online because each of them is an outstanding ethical leader.

While we are starting our conversation, and I will be using the moderators' prerogative of doing the opening questions myself, I want all of you in the audience to be thinking about questions as well. Beth will be monitoring the chat, and that is where you should type in your questions, and she'll be able to convey those to me during the event. So after I've done a few questions of my own, we will open them up to questions from you. We definitely want you to be part of this conversation. So without further ado, let me tell you who we've got with us here today on this incredible panel.

First of all, we have David Suzuki, legendary environmental activist, and for those of you who follow the Inamori Center, you may also recall that he was our 2012 Inamori Ethics Prize winner. It's wonderful to see you again, David, welcome back. Next we have with us Hans Cole, who is joining us from Patagonia where he is the head of environmental campaigns, grants, and activism. Another connection to our Inamori Ethics Prize, in 2013, our prize winner was Patagonia founder Yvon Chouinard. Good to see you, Hans. Thanks for joining us.

Next we have, from right here in Northeast Ohio, Jacqueline Gillon. She is the community engagement specialist and diversity coordinator for thriving communities Western Reserve Land Conservancy. She's also the co-leader of Black Environmental Leaders. Good to see you, Jackie. Last, but certainly not least, we have two of our own from Case Western Reserve University. First we have Ina Martin, who is the operations director of the Materials for Opto/electronics Research and Education, or the MORE Center, and also Stephanie Corbett, who is director of energy and sustainability and interim University Farm director. Ina and Stephanie are the co-leaders of Culture Change for Climate Change. Welcome to all our amazing panelists, and thank you for being with us here today.

Without any more introduction, I want to get right at it because this time is going to fly by, as it always does in events like these. I would like to launch my first question, if I may, at you, David. In your work for climate justice, you've made a point of reaching out respectfully to indigenous populations, such as the First Nations in Canada, to bring in and also prioritize their voices and perspectives for part of the conversation. You've also emphasized the importance of speaking with elders and having more intergenerational dialogue. Can you talk to us about why these things are important?

SUZUKI: Well I think we're at a critical point now where we desperately need to see our relationship with the world in a different way. You may have seen just yesterday that Sir Partha Dasgupta released a big report in Britain showing the way we evaluate economic success through the GDP is absolutely flawed and is in fact driving us in a very dangerous way. That is, it fails to incorporate the role that nature actually plays in keeping the planet habitable for us. If we destroy a forest that injects jobs and money into the economy, but that doesn't take into account what we've lost through the natural services that those forests perform, as long as they're intact and healthy.

For me, I became involved in the environmental movement in 1962, when Rachel Carson published *Silent Spring*. I was a geneticist. I thought I was a hotshot scientist, and suddenly this book came out, and I thought reading her book, the problem was people are taking too much stuff out of the environment and putting too much waste and stuff back into it. So we had to regulate that, but it was five or six years later, I realized we don't know enough to do that. It was when I did a film with indigenous people on an Island Archipelago off the tip of Alaska, and I said to this young Haida, Carver, I said, Why are you fighting logging? I mean logging is giving your people jobs. Many of the loggers are Haida. Why are you fighting the logging, what difference does it make to you when they destroy or cut down the forest? He said, Well yeah, we'll still be alive, but then we'll be like everybody else. I thought what the heck is he talking about, and then as I thought about it I realized that to him being Haida, who he was, his place on Earth, is told to him by his connection with the air, the water, the plants, the animals, all of that is what makes them who they are. When you destroy a part of that, they lose a part of who they are, and that led for me to see the environmental crisis in a very different way.

I think our problem is now, we have elevated ourselves as if we are the center of everything. The action is all about us, and environmentalists come along and say why you gotta be more careful in the way that we interact. What the indigenous people tell us is we've got it all wrong. We aren't the center of the action. We are a part of a complex web of relationships with all other species of animals and plants and air, water, soil, and sunlight, and we are able to live and flourish as long as that web is intact and abundant and generous to us. In that way of seeing ourselves, there is a fundamental reciprocity that in accepting nature's abundance in generosity, we have responsibilities to do everything we can to ensure that web remains intact and flourishes.

That's what comes to us from an indigenous perspective, their drive for the land is not only to protect what their lives get from that land, but to fulfill their responsibility to care for that land as well. I think we've got to look at our judicial systems, our economics systems, our political systems that are all built around us at the center. It's all about us, and we've got to find the way of seeing our relationship with the rest of creation on this planet in the way that indigenous people do.

FRENCH: I have to say as an ethicist that speaks to me very powerfully because so many times when I'm trying to get to the heart of unethical behavior and what has gone wrong, it boils down to that loss of perspective and the centering of oneself, that the ego coming first, and just the inability to recognize other impacts of our actions beyond ourselves. It's very powerful.

SUZUKI: One of the most powerful important words in my involvement with indigenous people that they taught me is, one, respect, that we can't exchange ideas if we don't have mutual respect for each other. The second word is reciprocity, that in accepting what nature gives us there is reciprocal obligation. One of the things that really worries me in North America is we've got this idea of John Wayne riding tall in the saddle and going out and pushing back the frontier and the rugged individualist, and when you look at how that manifests itself today, it's you know freedom, I want to be free. You look at the anti-vaxxer, they think that they're free. I keep saying to them, Wait a minute now, the air you're breathing out is going straight up my nose. Don't you have a responsibility? You don't have the right to wear or not wear a mask as if somehow you know this is an expression of your individuality. We don't have that sense of reciprocity that in living here and being in a community, we have responsibilities, as well as the right to be free and rugged, That's something that infuses so much of conversation in North America today. Freedom, you know I want to be free to make my own decisions. Well there are responsibilities that come with that kind of freedom.

FRENCH: I also find it funny in a bit of a sad way that a lot of the language that you're describing there, that freedom-based language, they will even harken back to pioneer spirit, things like that, without any acknowledgment that no one who was trying to be a pioneer could have survived without others, that anything that was achieved in those times that they're holding up as rugged individualism was actually not done by individuals alone, but by community supporting one another and without that is it all would have failed; we all fail if we don't work together and see that web. I really appreciate that point.

With that I think a nice connection can be made to another way in which we are not necessarily listening to all the voices that we should be listening to. Jacqueline, if I can bring you into the conversation, the US environmental movement has not historically centered people of color, and this is despite the fact that they played a significant role from George Washington Carver to Dr. Robert Bullard and so many others, the failure to acknowledge these contributions, plus the lack of diversity and representation, strike me as harmful since they're keeping vital voices and ideas out of the core conversation. As a Black environmental leader in Ohio, you've done a lot in our region to try to reverse this trend, and I'm curious, Do you see any signs of progress? What gives you hope that the climate justice movement is becoming more inclusive?

GILLON: That question is significant because it harkens back to what David is talking about, and he's talking about our humanity. First of all the acceptance that Black, indigenous, people of color are part of humanity, and humanity has to be in a powerful relationship with nature. But when you deny humanity, when you deny Black people's right to land and clean air and water, and deny the indigenous people their basic rights as human beings connected to the earth, you'll lose in the end. We're in place right now where we really have to spend a lot of time raising awareness and teaching not just others that don't look like us, but ourselves, because we've become isolated from the conversation though we've been a contributor for decades. The isolation is real, and we have to deal with that.

FRENCH: Thank you, and it's interesting isn't it, talking about isolation particularly in our current situation with the pandemic, which again connects to David's point about the expanding crisis that has been the COVID pandemic, was made worse by people not cooperating and not taking care for the reciprocity that is required of us as ethical beings. I find that very important as well. Ina, I'd like to bring you in here because of a connection that I just heard in what Jacqueline was talking about. I know that you and others at Case Western have been working on the Culture Change for Climate Change project and that brings in the neighborhoods near our campus. Again an artificial divide that can happen, used to be called town and gown between universities, or the ivory tower. What are the goals for that Culture Change for Climate Change effort and how does it focus beyond the university? What are you doing to work with people from the neighborhoods near our campus?

MARTIN: Great question, Culture Change for Climate Change is one of eight initiatives that was funded in 2020 by the provost's office at Case Western and the mission is to connect, promote, and create initiatives that are going to combat climate change and promote climate justice, not just at Case Western but with our neighbors. The idea is to—our goal really is to harmonize and scale climate action, and the approach that we have is a networking approach, so we're not building a new institute or a new center, but we want to be able to do is bring together people, both at Case, students, faculty, staff, and our communities to talk about how we can do more together. One of the really neat parts of this process has been getting to meet Jacqueline, and I'm looking forward to a lot more a lot more conversations with her.

So we started with this core team of organizers: there's myself and Stephanie, and also Grant Goodrich from the Great Lakes Energy Institute, Julian Rogers who's in the local government and community relations office, two sociology professors Cassie Pittman Claytor and Brian Gran, and physics professor and former dean of College of Arts and Sciences Cyrus Taylor. This is already a pretty broad-reaching group of people at the university, and the idea was we want to do this work on campus that's effectively just lowering the energy level for people to interact with each other across schools and departments on matters of climate change in climate justice. There are a lot of people working on this, there's a lot of great work being done on campus, around campus, between campus and the communities as well together. But we want to look at ways that people can build and expand on what they're doing. How do our political scientists and our engineers and our physicists and our philosophers all work together to be able to do more? Part of this effort and part of how we are currently working with the communities, it has to do with where we're starting. We talk about how we meet people where they are. Well where we're starting in terms of perceptions of climate change and possibilities for climate change action work in climate justice, that's a really varied space. It's not just a point, there's a lot of different people in a lot of different places, so one of the critical components to the Culture Change for Climate Change effort is actually a research project that's being led by the sociology professors and the physics professor, and what they're doing is designing and conducting focus groups in the communities to establish that baseline of what people's attitudes and perspectives are toward climate change. The idea is that conversations which will help us identify the themes that can be used to inform our longer-term actions so that we don't want to just jump in and start, so we want to figure out where we are, what's going to be useful, how do we foster these relationships, and then how do we then use that information to foster effective action.

FRENCH: Wonderful. I'm hearing a lot about relationships, about partnerships, about working interdisciplinary on all of these problems and bringing together groups that might not otherwise be part of these conversations. I'd actually like to bring in Hans Cole here because, I don't have to tell you this, that oftentimes when people are talking about environmental issues, corporations are the bad guy, painted as the villain of the piece and with some reason, there's a lot of examples we can give throughout history. And yet Patagonia, as an example, is actually held up the other way as an organization that has shown how to remain profitable while keeping the focus on sustainability, which is always been something that Yvon Chouinard has deeply believed in and making it a priority not to contribute further to environmental harm. Is this a model that other for-profit companies and corporations can follow, or is there something unique about Patagonia?

COLE: Thank you, Shannon. I appreciate the question, and it's an honor to be here on the panel. I'd say that absolutely this is a path that other companies and corporations can follow and in fact, it's not only one that they can follow it's an absolute imperative that other companies and corporations join this movement to think about more than just profit. To think about, as David was saying earlier, to move beyond measures like GDP and really think about the planet and people and the intersection of those two things. Patagonia certainly has some advantages I think when it comes to being a privately held company, we have some freedom to do what we want, so we push it, we push it to the very edge as much as we can, but there's some great models out there that companies can use to start to move down this path towards greater sustainability and towards greater responsibility. We're a B-corp, which means that we've incorporated some of these values and ways of thinking into our bylaws, and that's something that other corporations can do. They can become a B-corp. We've helped found groups like 1% for the Planet and the Conservation Alliance that are groups of companies that pool their resources and their funding to support good things. Certainly on climate in particular, there is sort of a baseline responsibility to reduce our carbon footprint, to do everything we can to reduce our impact on climate. We are looking to be 100% powered by renewable energy by 2025, I believe, in our US-owned and operated operations, we're really pushing hard on those fronts. I guess what I would say, too, in terms of the theme of the panel today is in some ways all that's just table stakes, that's just good hygiene for a company. Those are things that every company should be considering doing and moving down that path.

On climate justice, I just wanted to bring it to that deeper theme for a moment. I think that there is a considerable amount of additional action that companies and corporations should be considering taking that goes well beyond the four walls of our offices and factories and supply chain. This is an area that may feel less comfortable to companies and corporations, but we must do it. I think we must join the effort that the other leaders on this call are a part of, and you know it may feel uncomfortable in many ways at first, and I think there's some critical steps. A lot of it begins with humility, which I think several others have touched on so far, and connecting with community and having relationships. Our first step with this has to be acknowledging the impact that we have had and are having, that businesses are part of this economic system that has not focused on justice and the environment, and instead solely on profit. We have to acknowledge that has brought incredible damage to communities. We have to be transparent about that and humble about that, and open to that reality and criticism. Secondly, and even more important I think, we have to listen and learn. I think we are at the very, you know even Patagonia, and I appreciate the compliments you gave earlier in terms of what we've done in the past, we're in the very early stages of understanding climate justice. We really are. We need to learn; we need to listen to frontline communities. We need to understand, try to understand what they're facing, and we come to this as privileged individuals for the most part, who don't feel the impact of the climate crisis as acutely in many ways. We come in with that humility, we need to listen and learn, hear the concerns, and then think about what we can do to be supportive. Perhaps we can fund and support frontline organizations. We're working with groups like Climate Justice Alliance, Uprose, Asia-Pacific Environmental Network, lots of incredible groups that focus and are led by individuals and people in those frontline communities. We can fund and support. We can bring those financial resources and we can also bring our voice. I would say that again this might be a bit of a shift for many companies, but we need to get better at stepping back and allowing the voices and elevating the voices of frontline communities to our social media, to our web and online resources. We've got these great tools at our disposal, and an incredible audience. Patagonia reaches 2-3 million people whenever we put a message out there, because those are the folks who are buying our products. Can we bring individuals and voices into that megaphone and that podium and give them you know the opportunity to share the really important message of impact that is happening at the frontlines. I think there are some steps, there are some basic steps that we all need to take as companies and corporations, and absolutely other companies are following and should follow those paths, but there's more to it as well. There's deeper work that we need to do.

FRENCH: Thank you, and I'm finding myself, that word, humility, is really resonating with me, and I'm finding myself thinking around how everything that we've talked about so far in this panel is reminding us in one way or another whether we should be humble in the face of nature itself, or the humility to recognize that it isn't all about us as an individual or even a single company or any organization, and that reciprocity that David spoke of and bringing different voices to the to the foreground, which we heard about already from Jacqueline and Ina, all of that is part of making sure that we make some changes. That we can't simply continue with the status quo and the same voices and the same powerful entities controlling all of this because clearly that's not led us down the right path and that way lies destruction, certainly.

With that in mind I actually want to bring in our final panelist Stephanie to connect this to another large-size entity. We know that there's an ongoing international conversation about the obligations of large developed nations, like the US, who contributes so much more to climate change and its negative effects than smaller and less developed nations, and yet the consequences are not felt as profoundly there as they are in the places that can least survive those changes. Those who are the most vulnerable are being hit the hardest. I'm wondering then if you could connect that to large research institutions like the one that you and I work at, Case Western Reserve University. Do universities like ours have an obligation similar to the kind of obligations that Hans was just talking about for Patagonia to do more to address our climate change footprint then maybe some others do because of the power and influence that we might have?

CORBETT: Yes, and thank you very much for including our efforts on this panel. I very much resonated with what Hans said from Patagonia's perspective in the hope that other companies will jump in. I feel really lucky to be part of a university community that has embraced the idea that we are statesman organizations and that we need to lead at the community level. Our former President Barbara Snyder signed our university up for an effort called the American College University Presidents' Climate Commitment, and she believed even though she wasn't a climatologist, she firmly believed that universities had responsibility to take action on climate. Even though we have the will from top leadership, that doesn't mean that it's easy or instantaneous to negate our entire carbon footprint. Very large research institutions like ours use more energy than our counterparts at community colleges or neighboring institutions. We have 1,300 research labs here on campus and they are doing world-changing research. Really, it's important. Research here in Ohio's electricity grid that still relies on burning fossil fuels. They're dirtier than electricity grids in other parts of the country means that there's this inherent carbon footprint tied to doing this great research, and there's no magic wand to immediately reduce that.

Our university has invested a great deal of money in making our one hundred and twenty campus buildings more energy efficient, and that has real local benefit, but we need to go beyond that. We can't meet these big hairy audacious carbon neutrality goals without our community and our neighbors. Some of the solutions that our whole region needs to invest in and look at together are mass transit, and further investment in mass transit of course, and grid scale renewable energy. Those as just two of many potential solutions to helping our carbon footprint will also bring more quality of life to our neighbors. I think that this operational conundrum of trying to get to carbon neutrality can also be one of the entry points for this conversation that we all want to expand on climate justice. We don't have great metrics right now on what climate justice for an institution like Case Western looks like. We measure our greenhouse gas footprint. We report on it publicly, and there are lots of other sustainability benchmarks and goals that we work on very diligently together, but what exactly should our public facing goals on climate justice be and look like. What we count and what we pay attention to with the numbers matters. It means it gets invested in and that people are going to work on it on a daily basis, but we need to have a new and deeper and very authentic conversation with our non-academic neighbors to determine what that success is going to look like.

FRENCH: Yes, and as you talk about these conversations with our neighbors, we're back to this point that it is all of us who will be affected, and if we're not including everyone in the conversation and in the looking for the solutions for these problems, we are all going to fail together. It's a classic we're all going to fall together, which makes me bring up something that is—I'd actually like to focus this question towards you, David, because of how long you've been working in this in this area.

I get frustrated by the fact that here we all are, and we are all obviously concerned and trying to do our best and trying to learn what more we can do, but none of us is needing to be convinced that there's a problem. Yet, unfortunately, we all know that there are people who still don't see the urgency, still don't recognize it as a crisis. When you were given the Inamori Ethics Prize back in 2012, I vividly recall you speaking about the urgency, and you gave an analogy about microbes multiplying and filling up a test tube, and not realizing until it was far too late that after a certain point, there's no reversing the process. The microbes will in fact run out of test tube and all be doomed. What I wonder if you could talk to us about is, first of all, How do we convey that urgency, and then as a related point, Has that point of doom already come and gone, or can humans in fact still make enough changes to stop some of the damage?

SUZUKI: I think the answer to that is we don't know. I just heard a lecture, yesterday in fact, where Peter Victor from York University was saying that the weight of all mammals, that's the elephants, the whale, everything, of the weight of all mammals, ninety-six percent of the weight is humans and our domesticated animals, that's cattle, pigs. Ninety-six percent is us and what we are using for our purposes. Four percent of the weight of mammals around the world are wild creatures. Seventy percent of all of the birds, the weight of birds, is poultry. We say this is the Anthropocene epoch, a time when humans have become the major factor shaping the chemical, biological and physical properties of the planet on a scale undreamed of by any other species ever in the history of life on the planet. We've taken over the planet. A million species of plants and animals are now right on the cusp of going extinct. We have no idea in terms of long-term sustainability what this means, but I can tell you that as a top predator on this planet, we are the most vulnerable as these systems collapse around us. I have no idea. I used to say that I feel we're in a giant car heading in a brick wall at a hundred miles an hour, and everybody in the car is arguing about where they want to sit. It doesn't matter who's driving the thing. Someone's gotta say, Put the brakes on and turn the wheel, but we're locked in the trunk, nobody's paying attention. I don't use that metaphor anymore. What I say is if you remember Road Runner cartoons, where Road Runner is being chased by Wyle E. Coyote towards a cliff, and then at the last minute Roadrunner turns ninety degrees and avoids going over, but Wyle E. Coyote has got so much momentum he goes right over the edge. There's that moment when he goes, Oh my god, I'm not on the land anymore, and then down he goes. That's where we're at.

Now is that then a reason to say, Oh, it's too late, we can't do anything? Well I think that it makes a big difference whether you fall five feet or five hundred feet, so what we're trying to do now is to find a ledge that's only five feet down, but we're over the edge, and we have no idea whether we are inventive enough to find our way out. Indeed, there are scientists now who are saying human extinction is imminent. It's, well—I don't want to name names cause you'll go to them and then that's pretty depressing. There are scientists that are saying we have very few years to live on as a species. I think the only important thing is we have to try, and trying means that we have to recognize we're not smart enough to keep, to pull out of this. I know that there are companies now that are inventing ways of removing carbon from the atmosphere and you start thinking in order to do something, do you know how many tens of thousands of these machines are going to be needed to make a dent in removing the carbon that's necessary? Maybe it would be simpler to stop putting out more carbon into the atmosphere as our highest priority, and then start regreening the planet so that the system we know removes carbon, trees, will be there to start to effectively removing. That's the big step is that we have got to reign in ourselves, and humans never existed at this point when we had to worry about the collective impact of our species, but that's where we're at now. Collectively, we are undermining the very things that keep us alive, the air, the water, the soil, biodiversity on Earth, and we know if we don't act collectively, we're just going to continue on the path that we are and it's going to be a long way down to the bottom of this chasm.

FRENCH: I got that image burned in my mind now of Wyle E. Coyote where his legs spin for a moment and, then he looks down and realizes there's nothing but air beneath him and then falls. I would definitely like if we could at least make that drop as you said fewer feet then maybe we have a chance. We have to work together collectively to do that, which actually makes me want to bring out something that I have had a conversation with Ina about. You've argued, Ina, that sometimes on this kind of point that David just made it isn't as productive to focus as he indicated, it isn't as productive sometimes to focus on individual choices, like whether I put a particular can in the recycle bin or not. Those actions matter, and we need to do all of them because again the scale is so large, but that we also need to make the kind of changes he was talking about on a systemic level. Changes that involve things like urban planning. Can you talk to us a bit about the potential impact that could come from more systemic changes? That seems to follow nicely on from what David is reminding us.

MARTIN: Absolutely. I mean this is really the difference between one person saying I'm going to drive less, and then thinking about organizations being able to encourage people to live close to work and teleworking, so there's a large group of people that are driving less. Or somebody saying, Do I buy an energy-efficient vehicle versus what are the regulations for energy efficiency and emissions in vehicles as they are designed. I'm a chemist by training, my research is based on working with solar cells, and then I've been listening to a lot of people recently including urban planners. There is a tremendous presentation at Sustainable Cleveland this year by Julian Agyeman from Tufts, and he's in urban planning, and he was talking about the concept of just sustainabilities and the thing about the scope of this work is that it's immense, and there's things that we can do now, there's things that we have to plan for, we have to make these, what are lowest hanging fruit, but then what are our multiple year plans. There's the work that can be done with for example greening community spaces that don't have a lot of green spaces and this is something that happens a lot along racial lines, particularly in the US. Then there's when new spaces are being designed, how do we make those spaces not only sustainable but usable to a broad group of people. How do we stop this isolation of different communities and as a result of things, like public health is affected by zip code, and zip code is related to race. These are the things that I learn listening to people like Robert Fuller who works in this area, so it is this really broad conversation. Ultimately a system is made up of individuals, I used to look a lot and say, Who are the people that are working on this. In matters of climate and in matters of justice, I think it has to become less about finding the few people that are working on this and finding out how every single one of us can incorporate this into the work that we do. What are the systems that we affect that we can push on to start getting this mass level change that's needed to get that 45% reduction in carbon emissions from the 2010 level by 2030, which is now less than a decade away. These are the kinds of things we need to do. This is a huge effort, and it's something that everybody needs to be thinking about what they can work on. It's not about whose responsibility it is, because it's everybody's at this point.

FRENCH: I'm encouraged by how these points are building on one another. What you've just said not only connects to what David was talking about, but takes us back a few moments ago to what Hans was saying about if you have a platform, use it, and what Stephanie was saying about universities are doing certain things, but they need to really leverage everything they have towards this. All of which is coming back to the points around what we need to do collectively and individually in order to survive. I am reminded, I'd like to bring you back in, Jacqueline, if I could, with what Ina was talking about. Sometimes, and I'm certainly guilty of this as an academic, we talk in more scientific terms or in more of jargony ways about things, and that doesn't necessarily get the message out as clearly as it should. I think it could sometimes alienate some of the groups, and we need to be part of this conversation. I'm wondering if you can say something to us about your work and why it's important to use the right language to engage with communities directly. How can we do a better job to connect some of the more abstract ideas, like big terms like climate change or global warming, to specific effects that people feel and have lived, like urban heat islands or increased childhood asthma. If you could speak about that, I'd like to learn from you.

GILLON: I think the things that we hold in common are trees and our bodies and our health, so if we focus on the fact that in Cleveland our tree canopy is very low, and there is a really ambitious plan to plant more trees, about 300,000 more trees. For an elementary school student or for a scientist, they may describe the planting of trees and the effect of it differently, but we certainly can understand the health benefits, the air quality, reduction of carbon, all the wonderful benefits that come from planting trees. That's one basic thing we can do together no matter what language we use, where we live. What's significant is the fact that intentionally where people of color have lived, where black folks have lived, there was an intent to make sure that trees were not there, that the air quality was not enough for us to not get sick. We have to undo some things, some attitudes, and some beliefs so that we can go into our core neighborhoods and support planting trees, creating green space where there has not been green space regardless if we think these neighborhoods are developable or not. We all deserve access to green space. That's got to be a priority, and how we teach that, the language we use being very definitive about what these terms mean is important for adults and for children, because we want our young people to carry this message as well, so we can plant the trees together here in Cleveland.

FRENCH: I definitely want to plant trees with you, that's a deal, but I also appreciate that the history matters here, and what you're pointing out is the interlocking of these injustices, that these inequalities are so closely linked, and that there was a decision made, there were many decisions made, to actually make things worse for certain populations like the Black urban populations, and that we are still paying the price and will continue to do so unless those are very intentionally addressed one at a time. I think that's important; we can't forget that redlining and getting rid of green spaces or not allowing them to be developed, that wasn't an accident. Those were choices and that injustice has a long, long legacy. That connects to my mind to Stephanie, I know that you and I have talked about stories. It's interesting we had a panel on the general topic of justice in October on which we had another of Inamori Ethics Prize winners, LeVar Burton, and he also spoke about stories being incredibly important for people to connect on issues that really matter on this level. The idea of finding stories that resonate with people seems to be an important challenge when we're trying to address issues of this magnitude to get people to be moved to care on that emotional level to care about something like climate justice. Do you have any thoughts on how do we find those stories? Why are they important?

CORBETT: So for me, I'm an animal lover, and I really care about the Indiana bat population here in Ohio that's in trouble. I know as somebody who's trying to be a changemaker that just because I love animals doesn't mean that everybody does, and there's some people who are going to be motivated in different ways. I had a great mentor, Holly Harlan, who is an industrial designer who started a group locally called Entrepreneurs for Sustainability, and she always said, You gotta meet people where they are, and most people will care about one of the pieces of sustainability. We always refer to sustainability as the triple bottom line, people, planet, and prosperity. When I'm trying to find a story or a trigger that's going to make somebody care, whether that's somebody in an institution where we're trying to change business behavior, or if it's one of my neighbors who I wish was not putting pesticides on their lawn, I'm going to start with something I think they might care about. Maybe they are a people person and they get really motivated by the plight of children who are sick: did you know that childhood asthma is exasperated in our neighborhood by us all driving to University Circle where Case Western is alone in our cars? If I'm trying to talk to somebody in one of our labs about their electricity footprint because they have very intensive equipment, and we want it to be turned off at night, I might talk about how power plants in our area in Northeast Ohio are contributing to heart attack or asthma rates. But for some people it's the prosperity or jobs that really moves them, it's the economy, so when we're trying to get people to recycle correctly, I want to make sure they know that we're recycling is one of the top five industries in Ohio. When you recycle correctly, you're helping to potentially create jobs. For my kids, it's the love of Lake Erie, so I'm going to try to convince them to not buy the Capri Sun that's disposable at the grocery store so that we don't see single-use plastics on our local beaches. When I'm also talking about the economy and kids, we like to talk a lot about the fact that California is not the number one state in the country for green schools, Ohio is. We have more green, LEED-certified schools from US Green Building Council than any other state in the country, and that's something that we can be proud of. Regardless of the part or the change that we want to see, the only way to know what story is going to move someone is through being in a relationship with them, so we keep coming back to this. We have to know each other, we have to know what that lever is, and sharing stories inside of our organizations and with our neighbors through conversation does more than just hopefully get somebody to recycle correctly, right? It can lead to these deeper paradigm-shifting changes we all want to see.

FRENCH: Thank you, and I am thinking now about sharing our stories if you ask other people to tell you theirs, you can also pick up on what they care most about. I think you've highlighted how that works and then we can take that information to find those threads that tie us together and keep us moving in the right direction. Go ahead, David.

SUZUKI: You're moderating, I'm sorry, but I do have something to say about this. I began, I didn't know it at the time, but I was a scientist trained as a scientist, but I was asked to do a series on television in 1962 on genetics, because that was my specialty, and I realized what a powerful tool this was to educate a wide audience about things, and I felt as science was by far the most powerful force that is shaping our lives. If you look at our media, if you look at a newspaper, you've got a section on politics, a section on finance, you've got the section on celebrity, on sports, but where is there a discussion about the impact of what science is doing in our lives? I thought, This is a powerful tool that we could use. Now even back in the sixties we called television The Boob Tube, and there was, we looked down on it as a medium of popularization.

My colleagues in science really encouraged me to get off television. It was a vulgar way of communicating, but I thought—I knew that it was a cesspool out there, but I thought that I would be like a jewel, my programs would glisten like a jewel, and people would pluck me out and they would savor it and they would be educated. I have discovered that when you jump in the cesspool, you look like a turd like everybody else. The reason is the way that that is used, and after I'd been on air for quite a while people would come up and, Oh that was a great show you did on breast cancer. I'd say Gee, we haven't done a show on breast cancer. "Oh, that must have been on Mary Tyler Moore," or something. People get it all jumbled up, but they know that I'm the pre–Science Guy. I wasn't Bill Nye, but that's who I was. Information gets all mixed up. We come to a time, then, I thought that I was giving good information so people could make better decisions in their lives. Well guess what, we have more information in a cell phone now then people have had in all of human history. You can get into the US records of virtually anything that's ever been published in the archives there, and what do we do?

What I find is people come up to me and say, That climate change, listen, that's baloney. Why do you say that? "I found a website that says there are PhD people out there saying that it's a hoax." What I'm finding is people scroll, and there's so much information out there, that they just roll to it until they find something that confirms what they already believe. They don't have to change their mind, they don't have to get informed, and this is the real challenge we face now. People get caught up in things like the Q-Anon conspiracy idea, and they get into a tunnel and they go down there and, my God, the places they go. It means that you just search till things come out that are where you want them to be. You don't want to have to face the reality of climate change, and I think this is one of the real challenges. What the hell is our education about if we don't educate people about what information is and quality information, who do you trust, how do you track down who's paying for this particular website, or whatever, but this is what we have to do now. This is a real challenge when you see, I mean we had nine and a half years of a government that was headed by Stephen Harper, who is a pre-Trump Trump, and he did everything he could to deny the reality of climate change, to shut off avenues of information so that he didn't have to face the issue as a politician, and this is what I think is one of the major crises we face now. We're paralyzed by an inability to get people to come together and realize this is an existential threat.

FRENCH: Absolutely, and I'm very concerned, on many levels, about what you're highlighting there that the tremendous flood of information and information sources that's out there, it is out almost as an attack against particularly young people, who that is their first, and in many cases only, experience of how to acquire knowledge is, I'm going to Google it. They don't know what sources are better than others, and they don't know what to do to verify sources, and this is a huge responsibility for educators everywhere. It absolutely doesn't matter what field you're in if you are an educator, critical thinking has to be central. Teaching people about things like confirmation bias, which you were talking about that if you want to find a particular answer you will be able to go out and find someone who will back it up, but that doesn't mean that it is a good and reliable and valid source. Until we can get more on the same page that way it does scare me. It does worry me a great deal. I also want to acknowledge that there's been a trend against expertise and that is part of this anti-intellectualism, "How dare you tell me something," with authority, and that is quite sad because throughout, again, human history, where we have accomplished anything great and important, we've needed people who became experts in their particular field to help drive that.

SUZUKI: I believe universities really have a special role to play. It's not an accident that in many countries, developing world, when a revolution happens universities are often the place that are the center point of those revolutions. Universities occupy a very special place in society. It's where scholars and thinkers and dreamers can come together and push the envelope of human thought, but of course that becomes very threatening because many of the ideas are threatening to the status quo. What society has done in its wisdom has granted tenure. I can tell you tenure was this unbelievable privilege for me. I live in the province where forestry, where logging is a huge part of our economy, and when I began to go out and oppose the kind of clear-cutting practices, this raised, and a lot of the members of the board of the university were forest company executives. The cry for me shutting me up and getting me off was unbelievable, but I had tenure, and that was an incredible privilege. I felt it was my responsibility to speak out. I think one of the problems we should always have that role of encouraging out there ideas that can be shared, but universities have become increasingly dependent on support and money that is coming from corporations. The corporate impact is unbelievable. The forest faculty here were down on my head like you wouldn't believe because they're being supported by all of the industries that many of us were opposing. Universities I think really have a—they've got—they must play a big role, as in a group of elite people, but I don't think elitism is a pejorative myself. I think that they, that the university, has got to re-examine the whole role that the private sector is playing on them. I've seen Harvard University continue practices that they should have dumped a long time before, but because there were companies within the university itself fostering that activity, and this is in molecular biology, they continued to support it. Universities have gotten themselves into this awkward position, but they should be places of leadership on many of these ideas and thank God there are people like Michael Mann and James Hanson and others that have been able to speak out because they're in universities.

FRENCH: I'm certainly grateful to have tenure myself and the idea of academic freedom to speak our minds, but we definitely have to be on guard against—just generally the profit motive driving everything, and whether that's in universities or any part of public life, politics, everywhere, when it's about profit and not about flourishing for all the people involved, you're going to start seeing this long-term damage accumulate even faster.

Now with that, I need to take some of our questions from our audience and the first one is for you, Hans, so if you don't mind, I'm just going to literally read the question, Hans, that has come in for you and here's what it says, It seems to me that larger corporations have the advantage of higher revenue streams and predictable sales forecasts which allow for investment into long-term renewable energy technology. What's being done or can be done to help the countless numbers of small businesses or even households reach carbon neutrality when they may not have the available funds on hand to make those kinds of long-term investments?

COLE: Thanks for that, it's a great question, and I agree, I think that there is, the challenge is to help resources flow in some new directions to enable different parts of our society in our economy to really participate in this transition from fossil-fuel, the old ways of doing things, toward greater electrification and clean energy and all the rest, and it really comes to this concept that we've been again learning about, and new to, but really embracing recently called "just transition," which is really bringing in this notion of—as we move, as we make this big shift, as we make all the changes that we know are absolutely necessary that justice is a part of that equation. I think a lot of it comes to where does the money get spent. In the US right now we just had this big change in our administration from several years under the Trump administration now into the Biden administration, and there is a great deal of hope, I think, that this new administration will bring a new way of thinking in terms of how that money flows in our next couple of big packages of relief funding that comes out, that there will be a focus on that money flowing to communities to dispersed energy projects in frontline communities and communities of color in the communities that are actually impacted the most by the climate crisis. We should be seeing solar projects and wind projects in urban areas that have traditionally borne the brunt of the fossil-fuel industry in terms of all the pollution and all of the climate impacts as well. Seeing that funding flow, from government, through better policy towards communities that really need it, I think is an enormously important thing that needs to happen. Corporations, companies like ours, and others that do have the resources can also think of creative ways to invest. We have a program at Patagonia called Tin Shed Ventures where we take some of the profits that we have as a business and put it towards small business investment. It's kind of a little venture capital concept that funnels money towards smaller creative, environmentally sustainable ideas whether they're about energy or about avoiding pollution, or whatever the concept might be, but I think other companies could follow this example and think of how to—even an investment sort of model—put money into small businesses that need that kind of jump start to get going and it would really focus in communities that need it. I think at the government level and also from corporations.

FRENCH: I find that helpful the idea that it isn't a single answer that we're going to need some government support for small businesses and even households as the questioner asked to want to make these changes and then also corporations who do have that power can channel it in those ways to help the people who have the will, but not the way to do these kinds of changes. The next question from our audience is directed at Jackie. Jackie, as I did with Hans, I'm going to read you the actual question that got sent in from our audience so here it is: Much like what has been shown with recent developments in medical research, historically ignored communities have indicated that lot of trust is lost because of our history of negligence in including them. My fear is that the conversation will not begin without some effort on our part in rebuilding trust in the first place. How do we as a society best approach conversations with our neighbors who have been historically ignored or harmed with regards to climate change, and how can we rebuild some of that trust?

GILLON: I really appreciate that question. I work with the Western Reserve Land Conservancy, and about five years ago there was a real effort to bring more people of color into the space around natural resources and to really organize. We ended up here in Cleveland with Black Environmental Leaders, and our group has a group of allies, people that are, everybody that's not Black is in that allies group, but my point is we move at the speed of trust. Our conversations are intentional about how we feel, just being honest as human beings, dealing with and leaning into our discomfort, because these are not comfortable conversations at all. I invite the person that asked the question and all of us to begin with one person at a time that doesn't necessarily look like you. We don't have to talk about anything complicated like climate change, but just to begin a conversation where we can discover our own humanity, I believe is the first step. Our allies group has changed and grown. We captured the attention of almost thirty white-led environmental organizations. We come together with them on a quarterly basis, as well as our affinity group of our Black environmental leaders. The idea is that we have to build trust, and that's one conversation at a time.

FRENCH: Themes again, the one conversation at a time, those individual stories that we tell one another, working together, humility, cooperation, all of these themes that keep coming up in each of your comments. I find them all together starting to point the way, so I appreciate the way that that's going. I like that. I have a question that is directed towards Stephanie. Stephanie, this is the question from our audience, How can we start a global campaign to ban plastics and go back to sustainable packaging for everything? Is that realistic? As an individual, I can't impact the use of plastics, but could we start a marketing campaign to end plastic use, kind of like the campaign to wear seatbelts. A group started that campaign and then later became law. It became the new norm.

CORBETT: Wow, that's an awesome question. I may punt and ask if any other panelists want to jump in at some point, but I will just say we have some amazing researchers at Case Western. If I had a chance to live another life, I would like to be an industrial engineer and get to design those new materials that we need so that we could kick the plastic habit. Going back to Ina's comments when she was talking about the design of our communities, this is something where an individual consumer choice at the grocery store isn't going to win the day, we really need a systems-wide approach and manufacturing responsibility to choose new materials and have a plan for materials end-of-life more of a cradle-to-cradle design approach in everything that we do. I do think consumer campaigns can be really meaningful, the seatbelt campaign is a great example of how to do that, but at this point we are so reliant on this quick fix and disposable nature of what we buy in the convenience plastics. Even now with COVID here in Ohio, in Cuyahoga County where we are, we were on the verge of having a plastic bag ban right as the pandemic hit and that got put on pause because those fears about handling materials that were coming out of people's cars and homes that might be contaminated. I think we found out those are unfounded. I think there are lots of two steps forward, four steps back on the plastics front because of COVID, and I will welcome other input from panelists who have big ideas on how we're going to kick the disposable plastics habit.

FRENCH: David, please jump on in here.

SUZUKI: I believe you've gotta make the word "disposable" the most obscene, disgusting word. If someone says I got this disposable, you cover your children's ears and say, That man, don't listen to him. The whole idea of disposability is feeding the economic machine. It's ridiculous to think that we can use something once and throw it away. It's not just plastics. We were wiped out by the World War II, we were incarcerated as foreign aliens, anyway that's a whole other story. As Japanese Canadians, we were incarcerated and kicked out of British Columbia at the end of the war, and we were very poor. I've worn blue jeans all my life because denim wears like iron, and it just horrifies me to see people's now buying brand new pairs of denim jeans, that for hundreds of dollars that are already ripped, like what the heck. I thought clothing is what you do to keep warm in the winter and cool in the summer and cover the naughty parts, but a fashion statement? I think the whole clothing industry has got a huge day of reckoning coming. This idea that fashion somehow is what pushes product, that you're going to just throw away when the next fashion comes in. Get rid of the idea of disposability.

FRENCH: I have to say, Hans, you will appreciate this story. David, when Yvon Chouinard was, as you've been in this position receiving our Prize, I was waiting on the curb with him for his driver to take him and his wife off to the airport. I took a misstep and the heel broke off my high-heeled shoe, and I expressed, natural dismay, "I loved these shoes, I guess that's the end of them." In perfect true to form, he said, Hang on a minute, went into his bag, pulled out some kind of wonderful glue, and right there on the curb sidewalk, fixed my shoe for me, and did a little reminder that it's just broken, you can fix it, you don't have to dispose of it, you can just fix it. I am proud to say I still have that pair of shoes, but what a vivid reminder that we go so quickly to, "Oh it's broken," "Oh it's disposable," "Oh that's the end of that," and we know that things are built with obsolescence intended into them and the idea of making that shameful seems very powerful. Hans, had you known of that particular story, or is that just one of many for Yvon?

COLE: That's one of many. David, I couldn't agree with you more, as the guy here from a clothing company, I could not agree more with what you're saying. Patagonia has been working on this where we got a program called worn wear, if you haven't checked it out yet, it's all about repair, reuse, resale, renting clothes rather than buying. If you need a ski jacket if you need it once or twice, don't buy a new one. We don't want that. I think there's a revolution that needs to happen.

SUZUKI: What we have to do is make durability one of the big selling points. After the war, we were very poor, but we moved to Ontario where it was really cold, and my parents had to buy me a coat. I was in the growth spurt and a year later I had outgrown it, so it went to my sister and when she outgrew it, went to my younger sister, and my parents would brag, This coat went through three children. That's no longer a bragging point.

FRENCH: This seems like something that gives me some hope and encouragement. Ina, you and I have talked about this a little bit, did you want to jump in on this point as well?

MARTIN: About the plastics I was going to say there's the things that we choose to use that are perhaps optional, but then there are the things that are essential, for example the medical industry uses a lot of plastics, and those aren't going to go away anytime soon. Things like IV bags and there are things that you can't just—have a canvas bag for, especially in medicine. There's also the technological piece of this, and as a university there's a lot that's done here and in other places to develop, like Stephanie said, new material so people think about biodegradable plastics, what are alternatives, what are lessons that can be learned from the way things used to be done and can those be reapplied to use more materials that don't get into the environment the way the plastics do, but it's not just an option to not have them in the world that that we live in.

Going back to the question that went to Hans, I wanted to make a brief mention that there's this Department of Energy industrial assessment center at Case that's headed by a professor in mechanical and aerospace engineering named Chris Dewan, and they offer free energy efficiency assessments to any qualifying manufacturing companies and water treatment plants within a hundred fifty miles of Case. It's an example of where the university can interface with the neighborhood, and this is in a really practical technological way. The research university has resulted in the establishment of this program that can then be used to help companies figure out, so these are small and small mid-size manufacturers, how can you impact emissions, how do you become more efficient, how do you lower your energy bill, it's sort of a win–win all around.

GILLON: If I can jump in as well. Workforce development is essential to all of this, so how we utilize our workforce, whether it's creating the end products of recycled plastics or how we use all these clothes that we like to throw away to create other things. I think there's a real opportunity to think about how we put people to work and how we develop their entrepreneurship as we look at reusing things we throw away.

FRENCH: Absolutely. You all aren't going to believe this, but we're almost completely out of time. I have a question that came in for David that I aim at you, David, since that was the way the questioner wanted me to, but I think you all might want to make a closing comment on it. It seems like a very apt broad question for all of you, so we'll start with David and then see if anyone else wants to add on. Here is the question, In Western society particularly, it seems that a huge problem in creating momentum towards climate action is that society doesn't generally reward actions for the collective good enough. Instead the biggest perceived rewards appear to be given to those who take or work only for themselves. The question that we have is, How do we shift that reward system so that we are instead turning the rewards towards people making these contributions for the good of all?

SUZUKI: That's interesting because all along the west coast of British Columbia, indigenous people had a program or a practice called potlatching. In order to potlatch you can't just say, Oh I'm going to throw a potlatch. You have to acquire a certain level of standing in the community so that you can throw a potlatch, and what you do in a potlatch is you give away everything you own. What you get from that is an increase in status in the people that I work with a lot because I have two grandchildren who are Haida, for the Haida people when they build, carve a totem pole, if you throw a potlatch you can carve a ring around at the very top. If you go into a community and you see a totem pole with three rings on it, wow, that is a really important person. You gain status, when you give away everything you say, Oh my gosh, but you get it back many times more, not just in standing. When I go out and catch a fish or catch five or six fish, the best one goes back to the guy that threw that potlatch. It gets returned through the actions of the community, but the most important thing is that you gain respect by that event. Of course when Europeans came here they said, Look at these savages, they don't have any idea even of ownership or property, and they banned it. It was banned for almost a century, and people went to jail because doing a potlatch was a part of who they were. They had them. They had the potlatch, and thank goodness it's been brought back now but of course they are still learning how to have a potlatch, but I think it's a fantastic model. I don't understand why, I find it an obscenity that we have people who are billionaires, what the hell is that? A billion dollars, that's such a monumental number, but why can't we when you achieve a certain status of economic value then start giving medals of some sort, bronze, gold, silver, platinum, or whatever you want. Give them the status. There's no way they need that money, so let that money go to society and give them the status and recognition they deserve, but this whole idea that we have to reward this on the basis that they're worth a lot of money. They say Jeff Bezos is on his way to becoming a trillionaire like what the? That is so disgusting an idea.

FRENCH: Where you literally couldn't spend it all in your lifetime you literally couldn't. Unless you did give it away, there's no other way to. I agree, and there's some ideas there. I'd like to hear briefly if anyone else would like to jump in on how we shift towards more of the potlatch idea or the idea of putting time, status, to contributing to the community and to caring about our collective good. Are there ways that we can do that? Go ahead, Ina.

MARTIN: There's a Pew Research poll that came out a couple years ago about how two-thirds of Americans think that the federal government needs to do more about climate change, and the younger you are, the more that happens across political aisles and in fact for the youngest people it's well over half on both parties that think that this needs to happen. This isn't exactly an answer to this question, but it's more than I think there's a lot of people that want to do work on climate action on climate justice. I think there's a lot of people that just don't know where to start, or they're doing something small, and they don't know how to expand that. That's part of why these conversations and these groups become so important because if we can sort of lower that energy to action, lower that participation, and we start providing more paths for people to be able to move forward I think that can be a really powerful thing. People do what they are rewarded for that is true, but I think a lot of people do care. People that have families care, and that they want to make sure that things are okay for their kids and for other people's kids. I don't think that's so far removed from our whole society. Certainly there are areas maybe, but I feel like there's still a lot of hope for action there, and there's going to be a lot of talk about this reciprocity at the three o'clock Beamer-Schneider Professorship conversation that's part of the Ethics Table. I hope the audience is able to see that in the chat, the link, and join for part of that.

FRENCH: I'm being told that I have cheated and kept us over time a little bit here, but I couldn't resist it cause the conversation was so valuable, and I've certainly learned a lot here today, but we will use Ina's note of hope as our closing comment, I think that's encouraging. I hope that everyone who has joined us here today has not only valued this conversation, but sees themselves as part of it, and will continue this conversation. All of our incredible panelists are, as you can tell from their comments, deeply committed to making sure that this is an effort that is collective and is inclusive so we want this conversation to continue long beyond today's event. Thank you for joining us and please keep an eye on the Inamori Center's website for future Conversations on Justice. Once again thanks to all our panelists, and I do miss the good old days where you would hear the applause, but I assure you, you all deserve it. Thank you so much for inspiring us here today.

Leading through Crisis
A Rationale for Hope

Suzanne Rivera

Prior to 2020, most ordinary academics were not called upon frequently to apply ethical principles like justice in their everyday work. When they did, these opportunities were limited mainly to decisions for which the consequences rarely felt like they posed life-or-death stakes. As an ethicist and specialist in science policy and regulation, I frequently used to be called upon to opine about questions regarding the justice principle as it relates to study design, clinical trial recruitment, and oversight of research programs. Occasionally, I would be drawn into an ethics consultation pertaining to a particularly thorny problem related to alleged regulatory violations, scientific misconduct, or matters involving the potential for reputational harm to my employer. Other times, ethical dilemmas would emerge in the context of campus politics, such as during a departmental search for a new colleague. While interesting and important, these moments typically did not pose risks that an error of judgment would cause immediate and grave consequences.

Then, I accepted the role of college president on January 31, 2020. I knew it would be a difficult job, posing many challenges. I imagined the usual demands placed upon leaders of academic communities, and I felt a deep sense of humility about all that I did not yet know about how to navigate the unfamiliar terrain ahead. How best to support student success? How to foster the thriving of faculty and staff? How to increase access and equity across the campus? How to better engage alumni in the life of the college? How to deepen and strengthen relationships between the college and the local neighborhoods in the city? How to juggle the various demands on my time—including my obligations to family? How to raise the funds needed for new initiatives? These were the questions I pondered as I prepared to step into my new role on June 1.

Along came the COVID pandemic in February, plunging many people into fear, grief, and daily dilemmas about whether to get their hair cut, see a doctor for a non-urgent procedure, or visit an elderly relative. By March, most colleges and universities had vacated their dormitories and moved all instruction online. By April, it was clear that students would not be able to return for the rest of the academic term. In May, most graduation ceremonies were celebrated online in a virtual format. By this time, it was clear to me that the job I'd been offered was not the job I would inherit. I prepared mentally to arrive at a campus in need of a leader who would be undaunted by the added challenges posed by this unprecedented public health emergency.

At the end of May, a national civil rights crisis began when righteous anger erupted in the wake of numerous cases of egregious and fatal police brutality against unarmed Black civilians, including the killings of George Floyd and Breonna Taylor by law enforcement officers. Together, the global pandemic that leveled cruel consequences inequitably and a national outcry about racial injustice resulted in dramatic changes to our social lives, municipal priorities, and civic organizations, including every institution of higher education.

As a consequence, leadership positions with institutional responsibility for the safety and wellbeing of others became exponentially more complicated and demanding. Amidst these choppy waters, I took the helm of a small liberal arts college located at the center of our nation's broken heart: the Twin Cities region of Minnesota.

Was it helpful to have had training in bioethics when confronting a global pandemic? Yes, undoubtedly. That knowledge and experience gave me the discipline and structure with which to evaluate options and perform risk/benefit analyses. I used the four principles of bioethics. I called upon my understanding of the limits of utilitarianism. I thought about the duties I had to the campus community, to my Board, to my loved ones. I summoned moral virtues, like courage and patience, but a crisis rarely permits enough slack to think theoretically. Indeed, leadership requires the practical application of principles without the luxury of hypotheticals. The consequences of wrong choices are too much to bear when the stakes are so high.

The college's leadership team and I worked through the summer to plan for the campus to re-open in fall with a myriad of public health precautions. We studied the scientific data. We assessed what other similar colleges were planning. We also ran financial models designed to inform the many cost-saving measures we would have to implement in order to reduce eye-popping deficits caused by lost housing revenue and unbudgeted expenses, such as COVID testing. At the same time, I delved deeply into the work of anti-racism and equity, engaging with student activists, with local leaders, and with colleagues at other colleges and universities to address the deep structural inequities that—though present all along—had been revealed in a new light to those who previously had the privilege to ignore them. Perhaps most vexingly, all of this work was made more difficult by the fact that ninety percent of human interaction had to move online in order to reduce the spread of the virus.

As a new president facing these challenges, I was at a significant disadvantage. First, I did not know the physical campus, the people, the job duties, or even the geographic surroundings. Everything was new and confusing to me. Much of the cultural "iceberg" remained below the surface, and I could not see it. Second, I had to make consequential decisions about controverted issues under intense time pressure and without the benefit of a reservoir of earned goodwill from the college's students, faculty, staff, and alumni. They didn't know me and had no reason to give me the benefit of the doubt about the soundness of my judgment or the values that guided my thinking.

Some of the decisions I made had adverse outcomes for certain members of the campus community. To avoid layoffs, we froze salaries and hiring, and we temporarily suspended retirement contributions for all employees. All senior staff took a pay cut. We allowed only six hundred students to move into our residence halls in order to reduce housing density. That required canceling housing contracts for another six hundred or so students who were left to find another place to live just a month before the start of the fall semester. It also meant a significant loss of revenue. We rejected urging by the state that COVID testing be reserved only for sick people and paid for asymptomatic screening of our campus population. We changed the academic calendar, splitting each semester into two modules in which each student would take only two classes. We did this for a variety of sound reasons but found the experience was almost universally reviled by students for its velocity and compression. We canceled athletic competitions, sitting out seasons that other schools in our conference were willing to play, and we shortened spring break to discourage traveling.

It is too early for me to look back with wisdom and say with any clarity what I learned or whether in retrospect these were the "right" choices. We are still in the middle of the pandemic, with the US recently marking the loss of 590,000 people to COVID and no coordinated national program for speedy and effective vaccination. In addition, residents of the Twin Cities are still in pain over the killing of George Floyd and—more recently—Daunte Wright—by police. I can share observations about the principles and frameworks that guided my thinking about how to lead through this very difficult time in our nation's history.

First, with a hard nod to my training as a bioethicist, are the four principles of bioethics: autonomy, beneficence, justice, and non-maleficence (1979). While each principle is important, those experienced in applying them know that they very rarely can be maximized equally. In other words, they sometimes seem in competition or like they may cancel each other out. For some dilemmas, increasing justice might reduce beneficence. Likewise, an emphasis on respect of individual autonomy might limit justice. An understanding that tough choices include trade-offs is difficult to accept, but it's necessary in order to move forward without being paralyzed by endless analysis. Accordingly, when I accepted the idea that—while there might be obviously wrong choices—often there are multiple good ones, it liberated my thinking about possible paths forward.

Not all the decisions I had to make this year would be considered strictly the purview of bioethics. Some were straightforward financial decisions made to preserve the economic stability of the college or logistical decisions made to reduce workload for people under a tremendous amount of stress. Nevertheless, these choices had ethical dimensions, and I found that the four principles of bioethics provided a reliable heuristic. Allowing faculty to decide whether to teach remotely (maximizing autonomy) might reduce the satisfaction and happiness of students (reducing beneficence). Also, remote teaching might not be fair as some students would not have access to reliable Wi-Fi or a quiet place to dial in for an online class (reducing justice). Forcing faculty to teach in person (reducing autonomy) might make some students happier (increasing beneficence) but expose students and faculty to higher COVID infection risk (reducing beneficence). Not all people are equally vulnerable to the disease, so allowing people to sort themselves by preference necessarily would yield inequitable health outcomes because of differences in privilege (reducing justice). Encouraging students to protest police violence supports their freedom of expression (maximizing autonomy) but might expose them and the rest of our community to the virus (reducing beneficence). Frequently it was the (arguably) most misunderstood bioethics principle, non-maleficence, that brought me up short: considering two or more less-than-ideal solutions, which inflicts the least harm? By what scale do we measure to compare the pain of potential lost lives against the material consequences of lost livelihoods?

The second framework that guided my leadership in this difficult year was the Stockdale Paradox. This is a concept made famous in Jim Collins's bestselling book *From Good to Great* (2001), which told the story of Admiral

James Stockdale, who was a POW during the Vietnam War. Stockdale survived, while many others did not. When asked why he thought that was so, he is quoted as having said, "You must maintain unwavering faith that you can and will prevail in the end, regardless of the difficulties, and at the same time, have the discipline to confront the most brutal facts of your current reality, whatever they might be." This particular brand of stoicism may not appeal to everyone but, as observed by Groysberg and Abrahams (2020), the Stockdale Paradox provides an especially useful way to think about the role of the leader in a crisis.

Per the paradox, an effective leader must be honest about the challenges they face, provide empathy about the consequences of those challenges, and offer a rational basis for hope that things can improve. Offering hope in the face of a lethal global pandemic and a national civil rights crisis is not easy. It doesn't mean ignoring the daunting realities we face in favor of a rosier outlook. It means naming the pain and grief caused by the virus, calling out racism and other forms of bigotry, being honest about the inequitable ways the virus affects underserved and marginalized communities, and inspiring belief in a realistic plan for moving forward. I use the word "forward" here deliberately as an intentional alternative to the notion of "returning to normal." If this year has taught us anything, it's that the old normal wasn't working well for everyone. In the old normal, social determinants such as zip code and skin shade could predict disparate healthcare outcomes, educational attainment, likelihood of incarceration, and infant mortality. In the old normal, we were guided more often by "we can't because" thinking rather than "we could if" thinking. When we are past the pandemic, we should not strive to return to that normal because it was unfair. Which brings us back to justice.

One new leader at one small college cannot undo generations of structural inequality that undergird our society. Nor do I have the skills to invent a coronavirus vaccine or cure. After this whirlwind of a year, I still have a lot to learn as a college president. But one thing I know is that all leaders in all sectors and at all stages in their careers have an opportunity right now to reject the comfort of familiarity when old habits uphold systems that do harm. Choosing to imagine a different future under challenging circumstances is what Thomas Homer-Dixon (2020) calls "fighting a scarcity of hope."

Despite circumstances that may temper our evolutionary inclination toward optimism, I do have a rational basis for hope that, if we see injustice, and we name it—with empathy about its consequences and clear eyes about what it will take to root it out—then, together, we can build an alternative vision for the future. We can create a new normal that retains and applies all the lessons we learned this year about inclusion and equity, about ingenuity, and about our tolerance for change. Indeed, we must do so.

Works Cited

Beauchamp, T., & Childress, J. 1979. *Principles of Biomedical Ethics*. New York: Oxford University Press.

Collins, J. C. 2001. *Good to Great: Why Some Companies Make the Leap…and Others Don't*. New York: HarperCollins.

Groysberg B. & Abrahams R. Harvard Business School. *What the Stockdale Paradox Tells Us about Crisis Leadership*. https://hbswk.hbs.edu/item/what-the-stockdale-paradox-tells-us-about-crisis-leadership. Accessed February 24, 2021.

Homer-Dixon, T. 2020. *Commanding Hope: The Power We Have to Renew a World in Peril*. Canada: PenguinRandomHouse.

Ethical Leadership in the Hidden Curriculum
What Contribution Would You Like to Make?

Gregory L. Eastwood

> *Leadership...is an essentially moral act.*
> —*A. Bartlett Giamatti, former President of Yale University and former Commissioner of Major League Baseball*

> *Being a physician inherently means that you are a leader.*
> —*Medical student, State University of New York, Upstate Medical University*

The hidden curriculum, that informal but powerful experience which permeates the explicit curriculum throughout all formal education, is an important influence in the development of a person's attitudes and behaviors. Through the hidden curriculum we observe the behaviors of teachers, coaches, others in authority, and sometimes peers, and they become incorporated into who we are and how we behave. This may be intentional, but often is not.

The hidden curriculum can be an effective tool for the development of ethical leadership. Although notions of ethical leadership may be somewhat intuitive, I offer that ethical leadership includes behaviors that reflect the character traits of integrity, honesty, trustworthiness, courage, respect, tolerance, humility, and perseverance.[1] Perhaps we can grasp the essential character of ethical leadership from the language that describes nominees for the Inamori Ethics Prize that is conferred annually by the Inamori International Center for Ethics and Excellence at Case Western Reserve University: "The nominee should be a person who has either shown or taught others what true ethical leadership is... [and whose] work should urge respect for the dignity and worth of all human beings, and he or she should inspire others to action."[2]

In the following, I first will review the hidden curriculum historically in general education. Then, because I am most familiar with the hidden curriculum in medical education, and it is in medical education that the hidden curriculum has been studied most extensively, I will describe more fully that expression of the hidden curriculum. Next, I will argue for the intentional use of the hidden curriculum to model and teach ethical leadership. Finally, I will pose the question to anyone who is involved in education and instruction of any kind: As you become more aware of the power of the hidden curriculum, what contribution would you like to make to the development of ethical leadership?

The hidden curriculum in general education

The hidden curriculum was anticipated over one hundred years ago when John Dewey, the philosopher and influential reformer of education, proclaimed, "[E]very social arrangement is educative..."[3] Dewey observed, with regard to the need for organized education in advanced societies, that "as societies become more complex in structure and resources, the need of formal or intentional teaching and learning increases." With growth of this formal curriculum of teaching, "there is the danger of creating an undesirable split between the experience gained in more direct associations" (i.e., with the behaviors of teachers and others through the hidden curriculum) "and what is acquired in school" (i.e., through the formal curriculum).

The first use of the term "hidden curriculum," however, came in 1968 when Philip Jackson described the hidden curriculum as "the norms and values that are implicitly, but effectively, taught in schools and that are not usually talked about in teachers' statements of goals."[4] Two years later, psychiatrist Benson Snyder, in his book *The Hidden Curriculum*, further defined the effects of the hidden curriculum in higher education.[5] He theorized that much of the anxiety and conflict that students experience arise from academic expectations and social norms that are not expressed explicitly and that may conflict with the content and stated expectations of the acknowledged curriculum.

In 2004, Michael Apple, as he observed the dynamics of learning in high school social studies and science classes, declared, "It is beginning to be clear that 'incidental learning' contributes more to the political socialization of a student than do, say, civics classes or other forms of deliberate teaching of specific value orientations."[6] He felt that children are taught how to deal with and relate to authority figures by the patterns of interactions they see in school.

As I have thought more about the importance of the hidden curriculum, not only in our education, but in the overall process of learning from young childhood, I am reminded of the aphorism, "Do as I say, not as I do."

Acknowledging the hidden curriculum and mitigating whatever negative effects it may have seems to be in our cultural DNA. "Do as I say" roughly represents the formal curriculum of growing up, but we learn also from observing the behaviors of our parents and teachers and others—what they actually do—in life's parallel curriculum. One of my students observed, "I tend to think of it as the same 'hidden curriculum' we all have growing up in our families."

The hidden curriculum in medical education

Medical students and residents in training learn the facts and content of medicine through the explicit curriculum in medical school and during residency. But it is through the hidden curriculum that they learn how to *be* a physician and express the attitudes and behaviors of being a medical doctor. In the hidden curriculum they observe the behaviors of their teachers and colleagues and either emulate them or decide to behave differently. Ironically, they can learn a lot about being a good doctor from examples of bad behavior simply by deciding to behave otherwise. The hidden curriculum can be a powerful force to develop collegiality, collaboration, and exemplary physician-professional behaviors; conversely it can be a pernicious influence to sow discord, disrespect, and negative behaviors. It also largely determines how physicians care for patients.

The hidden curriculum in medical education came out of hiding over twenty-five years ago when Hafferty and Franks first described the role of the hidden curriculum as a major means by which medical students and other trainees learn how to be physicians.[7] They said, "...most of the critical determinants of physician identity operate *not* within the formal curriculum but in a more subtle, less officially recognized 'hidden curriculum.'" Since then, hundreds of studies and reports on the hidden curriculum have appeared, further describing it, documenting its role in the formation of practicing physicians, and studying how it might be used intentionally to improve medical education and thereby produce the "good physician."

Physician and medical writer Pauline Chen, says,

> While most of medical education and training is about the nuts and bolts of clinical care—how to treat hypertension, how to manage a ventilator, how to take out a gallbladder—the process also involves learning how to *be* 'a doctor.'...Medical students copy the lingo, manners, and expressions of more established senior residents and attending physicians. The lessons from these

role models, who are often tired and stressed out themselves, can be sobering…Even established physicians can be re-inspired to adopt new humanistic skills, becoming better teachers and role models in the process.[8]

I teach in a bioethics course as a faculty leader of about fifteen medical students who meet every several weeks, twelve times throughout their third year of medical school. We discuss a particular topic each session, such as "Respecting Patients While Learning on Them," "Physicians' Responsibilities to Patients at the End of Life," and "Access to Health Care." Towards the end of the course the topic for one session is "The Hidden Curriculum," although the hidden curriculum arises implicitly during every session when students describe their observations of the behaviors of physicians, residents, nurses, and other health professionals. As part of the discussion on the hidden curriculum, students respond to the following questions:

1. Describe a personal experience you have had with a positive example of the hidden curriculum. (This may be something that you want to emulate and think is characteristic of a good physician.)
2. Describe a personal experience you have had with a negative example of the hidden curriculum. (You probably don't want to do this.)
3. As your training progresses (i.e., in medical school and residency), what contribution would you like to make to the hidden curriculum?

Here are some positive examples of the hidden curriculum:

"The chief resident took as much time as was necessary to explain to patients exactly what was happening and make sure all questions were answered."

"I watched a psychiatry fellow develop rapport with a fifteen-year-old girl who had been experiencing suicidal ideation. The connection I saw him build was tangible."

"After the failed resuscitation, the resident and I left to continue rounds. He turned to me and asked if that was the first death I had ever witnessed and asked me if I was OK. He gave me time to reflect and discuss what I had just witnessed."

Some negative examples:

> Regarding a contentious interaction between a physician and a
> nurse practitioner: "The NP refused and stated this was not her
> job. The two continued to argue. The NP refused to see any of
> my preceptor's patients. My preceptor said, 'I am an attending,
> you are a nurse.'"

> "My resident said, 'Don't follow that patient. There is nothing
> to learn. It's just a psych patient.'"

> "My resident asked another resident if the patient who had been
> difficult to work with was Black."

The responses to the first two questions always are interesting and gener-
ate robust discussion, but the genius of this exercise is in the third question,
"As your training progresses (i.e., in medical school and residency), what
contribution would you like to make to the hidden curriculum?" This
commits the student to responsibility for the hidden curriculum largely as
a teacher and one who can set an example.

In responding to this question, students universally acknowledge the existence and the power of the hidden curriculum and that they are important
players in it, both as learners and as teachers. Although many responses seem
student-focused, indicating a commitment to behaving in ways that improve
the teaching and well-being of medical students, and other responses commit
to using the hidden curriculum to improve the care of patients, still another
important theme is leadership and related notions of setting an example.
Students are aware that when they are residents and attending physicians,
future students will be observing and learning from them.

Students accept that they have influence over others in various ways and
express their intent, as they progress through their training, to practice
integrity and honesty, serve as a positive role model for students, and be a
good mentor. This is what some students say:

> "Being a physician inherently means that you are a leader. People
> look to you to be professional, conscientious, competent, and
> deliberate."

> "I'd like to be a leader that students look up to. To show patience
> in the face of frustration, to listen when the conversation becomes
> heated."

> "You should lead by example."

Their example includes practicing good behaviors, such as being respectful of all patients regardless of social status, ethnicity, demeanor, or disability and of others on the healthcare team; being a good communicator and listener with students, colleagues, and patients; and being reliable and patient.

The intentional use of the hidden curriculum to model and teach ethical leadership

In the preceding I have tried to show that the hidden curriculum is real and effective in teaching us how to think and behave in our educational milieu. This type of learning begins in childhood and continues throughout the chronological range of formal education. It not only serves to adapt us to the educational environment itself, but also, in the example of medicine, it largely determines the behaviors in one's professional development. Thus, it is through the hidden curriculum that we perceive most of the behaviors relevant to our educational and professional environment. These behaviors that we observe in others and adapt to ourselves largely are appropriate and beneficial, but some are not.

You may have noticed that I mention "behaviors" a lot and have not emphasized "thoughts" and "attitudes" and other indicators of mental activity. So, before we go further, let me explain my ideas about thoughts, attitudes, motivations, and behaviors.

What comes first, good thoughts, attitudes, and motivations—that which goes on in our minds? Or is it good behaviors—that which is evident to others? It seems intuitive that our thoughts should drive our behaviors. Yet, Aristotle reminds us that our behavior can change our thinking. He says that by doing just behaviors, such as acting virtuously or courageously, we may become more virtuous or courageous.[9] It seems that behavior and thinking influence each other by some sort of feedback loop. What may be more important—thoughts or actions—may depend on context, but Aristotle seemingly would give the edge to behavior.

To use the practice of medicine as an example, also apparently would patients and society. We want our doctor to be empathetic, honest, knowledgeable, committed to our welfare, and the like. Since we do not have direct access to our physician's thoughts and motivations through some kind of telepathic probe, these characteristics are inferred by the physician's speech, body language, and other actions, which I classify as behaviors. Further, I observe that none of us has direct access to any other person's mind. We gauge another person's thoughts, attitudes, and motivations through their behaviors of speech, writing, body language, and other actions. This not only is true for people we interact with infrequently, such as our automobile mechanic, a clerk in a store, and even our dentist or physician, but it also seems true for those with whom we may be more familiar. How else do we know the thoughts, attitudes, and motivations of our intimates except by listening to them speak, observing their facial expressions and movements, reading their texts and emails, and experiencing their interactions with us and others, all of which I regard as behaviors? That is why I emphasize behaviors and hope that if we can change behaviors, the mind will follow. And perhaps we can teach ethical leadership, with a nod to Aristotle, by teaching right behaviors. Moreover, relevant to the notion that the hidden curriculum is a powerful influence on developing current behaviors, I believe that current behavior is a dependable predictor of future behavior and that the link between the present and the future is one of moral character and associated behaviors.[10]

Let us return now to the notion of using the hidden curriculum to model and teach ethical leadership. I suggest the following:

1. Acknowledge the power of the hidden curriculum to influence behaviors in others and that you play an important role in it, both as a teacher and as a learner.

2. Be aware that you are "on stage" most of your professional life, that you are modeling a range of behaviors, and that others are learning from your exemplary behaviors as well as those that are less admirable.

3. Be attentive to the behaviors of others and be open to learning from them, whether they are your students, your peers, or your teachers and mentors.

4. Call attention to the hidden curriculum so that it becomes better understood, less hidden, and more related to the explicit curriculum.

5. Take the limitless opportunities offered by the hidden curriculum to promote ethical leadership. This requires, as you become more aware of the power of the hidden curriculum, that you think about the following:

What contribution would you like to make to the development of ethical leadership in the hidden curriculum?

References

1. Eastwood, Gregory L. How Literature Informs Notions of Leadership. *Journal of Leadership Education* 2010; vol. 9(1):173–189.

2. Inamori Ethics Prize Nomination Form. https://case.edu/inamori/inamori-ethics-prize/prize-nomination-form.

3. Dewey, John. 1916. *Democracy and Education: An Introduction to the Philosophy of Education.*

4. Jackson, Philip. 1968. *Life in Classrooms.* New York: Holt, Rinehart & Winston.

5. Snyder, Benson R. 1970. *The Hidden Curriculum.* Alfred A. Knopf.

6. Apple, Michael M. 2004. *Ideology and Curriculum,* 3rd ed. Chap 4. *The Hidden Curriculum and the Nature of Conflict.* Routledge Farmer.

7. Hafferty, Frederic W. and Franks, Ronald. 1994. *Hidden Curriculum, Ethics Teaching, and the Structure of Medical Education.* Acad Med 1994; vol. 69: p. 861–871.

8. Chen, Pauline W. 2009. "The Hidden Curriculum of Medical School." *New York Times,* January 29, 2009.

9. Aristotle. *The Nicomachean Ethics, Book II.*

10. Eastwood, Gregory L. 2013. Moral Choices and Leadership. *International Journal of Ethical Leadership* 2013; vol. 2: 121–135 (Fall 2013).

What Senior Leaders in Defence Should Know about Ethics and the Role That They Play in Creating the Right Command Climate

Prof. David Whetham
Director of the Centre for Military Ethics, King's College
London[1]

Introduction

Ethical leadership encompasses both the personal conduct of the leader and the leader's expectations that followers behave ethically.[2] This paper explores some of the principal reasons that ethical failures occur and, just as importantly, what practical steps military leaders can take to prevent them from happening. It draws on published doctrine, operational experience, academic research, scientific reports, and inquiries such as Chilcot (the Iraq Inquiry) and the Op Telemeter Internal Review (focusing on "Marine A") to examine everything ranging from the psychological causes for certain behaviours, to the way that our environment shapes the way we see the world around us. It will also explore how nurturing the right leadership environment can foster and promote good behaviour at both an individual and organisational level. While this is intended to provide guidance for leaders across defence, it finds inspiration in the Army Leadership Code, which draws on both historical and contemporary experience to list seven leadership behaviours.[3] These behaviours provide a useful framework for discussing what leaders can do to create and support an appropriate ethical climate within defence.

- Lead by example
- Encourage thinking
- Apply reward and discipline
- Demand high performance
- Encourage confidence in the team
- Recognise individual strengths and weaknesses
- Strive for team goals

The challenge, of course, is not coming up with a list of helpful principles but understanding what they mean in practice and working out how to actually apply them. It is useful to look at both good examples and best practices, but also to examine and understand how and why failures have occurred.[4] This paper will therefore refer to both the good and the bad to illustrate the points being made.

Lead by example

Taking command is normally considered the high point of a military career for those who are privileged to be entrusted with it, but leadership is something that is expected across a wide range of roles in defence. Clearly there is a relationship between leadership and power, and it is therefore useful to start with the observation that power can (or may) change behaviour.

The military invests a huge amount of effort in ensuring that those they promote into positions of authority have the character to be able to rise to the challenge of their new position. Such focus on character begins at officer selection and is then a recurring theme as the different values and standards are internalised through conscious training and unconscious institutional diffusion.[5] The British military is not unique in relying heavily on a virtue ethics model that would have been very familiar to Aristotle.[6] Virtue ethics concentrates on the importance of character and on how we can nurture the right types of behaviour by practicing what we should do. The more we do the right thing, the more it becomes habit and therefore part of the stable disposition that informs one's character. While stated as values rather than virtues, the different services provide institutional articulation of expected behaviour. They hope that, by fostering such behaviours and promoting those who consistently demonstrate them, people will be able to do the right thing when the situation demands it.[7]

Ethical leaders understand that their own character is an important resource to draw upon, but also that it may not be sufficient to protect themselves from being affected in a negative way by their situation. Only by understanding the effects of the environment on our perceptions and behaviours can we be confident of acting correctly despite the temptations and opportunities around us. Command brings many kinds of power, and while the link between power and ethical behaviour is multifaceted, we know that power can corrupt. It increases disinhibition, which itself fosters selfish behaviour. This can include acting in ways that gratify individual desires or giving into temptation. For example, people in positions of power are more likely than others to lie, cheat, and engage in infidelity.[8] In an influential piece from 1993, Ludwig and Longenecker argued that embedded in success may be the very seeds that can "lead to the downfall of both the leader and the organisation."[9] Amongst other things, success and promotion can lead to a change in perception of one's own abilities and can contribute to an inflated belief in one's personal ability to control outcomes. After all, you got where you are because you're good, right? One of the ways to avoid this type of hubris is to build a team of people that you can trust and empower them to be able to provide challenge or comfort when you need it. These will be people that can robustly (but quietly) criticise or correct as required, and might be your executive officer, a mentor, peer, or trusted friend. The chaplain or padre often provides a spiritual resource for military units and may also be able to provide assistance in this role as someone who can provide a detached perspective. The important thing is not who the person or small group of people are, but that they are empowered by the leader to challenge him or her whenever it is needed to provide a sense of perspective.

One thing that seems to be consistent across leadership, be it civilian or military, is that many people unfortunately wear their sleep deprivation as a badge of honour. Sleep allows us to consolidate and store memories, process emotional experiences, replenish glucose (the molecule that fuels the brain), and clear out beta–amyloid (the waste product that builds up in Alzheimer's patients and disrupts cognitive activity). By contrast, insufficient sleep and fatigue leads to poor judgment, lack of self-control, and impaired creativity.[10] On top of this, sleep deprivation also increases the likelihood that people will engage in unethical behaviour.[11] For example, in one study carried out at the Norwegian Military Academy, extremely sleep-deprived students on a training exercise were expecting to fire on non-human dummies. When the targets unexpectedly turned out to be real people, fifty-nine percent of students still fired their weapons in response to an order when it was clear that they should categorically not have engaged (thankfully their rifles were disabled for the exercise).[12] Although extreme sleep deprivation clearly impacts ethical behaviour, researchers have found that lower levels of fatigue can also have a negative influence.[13] For example, some researchers have found that people act more ethically in the morning than in the afternoon, a finding dubbed the "morning moral effect."[14]

What can you do about it? While sticking to a fixed schedule to ensure sufficient rest may not always be an option, if your staff understand how important it is, it should be possible to manage time more efficiently to create rest opportunities. Mindfulness exercises and restricting caffeine intake in the hours before sleep can both help, while even a twenty-minute nap can speed up cognitive processing, decrease errors, and increase stamina.[15] It is clear that you appear to have more time to do more work if you sleep less, but any extra productivity is often an illusion and is likely to affect the whole command, not just your own decisions and awareness. Your leadership, whether good or bad, affects the moral identity of those around, above and below through the example that you set. Leaders who discount the value of sleep can negatively impact wider behaviours on their teams as those under them pay close attention to cues and adjust their own behaviour accordingly. Conversely, if your people see that you take being appropriately rested seriously, they are more likely to take it seriously themselves. This is probably the single most effective thing that any leader can do to foster ethical resilience in any organisation.[16]

Encourage thinking

Absolute certainty is not always the strength people think it is—sometimes it is good to question and be questioned. Admiral Woodward demonstrated this in 1982 when he chose not to shoot down an aircraft approaching the British fleet with an apparently hostile profile and on an intercept course, despite having both the Rules of Engagement (ROE) and legal permissions to act. Thankfully, rather than simply authorising weapon release for when the aircraft crossed the defensive perimeter, the admiral carried out one last check, asking for the origin and destination point of the incoming aircraft to be quickly plotted. According to his diary, with only twenty seconds to spare, this last check resulted in the answer that the aircraft was on a direct line running between Durban and Rio de Janeiro—obviously a flight path that was very likely to be used by a commercial airliner. The decision to wait was confirmed when the fleet's Harrier finally came close enough to confirm that the aircraft was a Brazilian airliner going about its normal business.[17] Our brains repeat patterns in order to make decisions more quickly, and they selectively seek out information that confirms what we already believe. While this can be often be very helpful, these mental shortcuts don't always lead to accurate conclusions. This situation was saved by the leader continuing to question himself, but JDP 04 (the Joint Doctrine Publication on "understanding and decision making") also warns us today that an over-reliance on a "specific technology, applications or bearers to deliver mission critical information, can lead to single points of failure."[18] For example, it is easy to see how machine bias means that answers generated by an artificial intelligence algorithm can be taken as definitive, even when they are very clearly wrong from any objective position (demonstrated every time we see someone driving into a river while following their satnav).[19] Some environments will be more challenging than others. For example, "perceptions and bias can be even more prevalent and entrenched when working with allies or occasional partners."[20]

As far as confidence in your own decisions goes, as well as being willing to question yourself, don't be afraid to be challenged. The disciplined obedience that must be maintained so that orders in the face of overwhelming danger on the battlefield will be obeyed without hesitation is too often used as an excuse not to listen to, or offer, alternative views when there is the time and opportunity. Inviting "reasonable challenge" is one of the best safeguards that any leader can have against their own hubris and can force you to think about your own motivations, but it is also an important corrective to certainty in wider contexts when it might be misplaced due to insufficient or inaccurate information, bias, or limited perspective.[21]

Following the UK's intervention in Iraq in 2003, the Chilcot Inquiry published its long-awaited report in 2016.[22] This made uncomfortable reading for the Ministry of Defence, highlighting significant failures in leadership, processes, and organisational culture. The inquiry identified a number of factors that led to these failures, including a disturbing tendency to "groupthink" across government, where people conformed in their thinking to such an extent that the decisions they made became dysfunctional or even irrational. Key assumptions were not questioned, even when those assumptions were blatantly false. As a response, the UK MoD has repackaged the idea of constructive dissent as "reasonable challenge." This is now being taught across the professional development courses taken at each promotion stage for all three services as a way of escaping a tendency towards groupthink. The policy document starts astutely by addressing those who receive the challenge, rather than those who might make it, and this is particularly important. Rather than just telling people not to be bystanders and encouraging them to speak up when they see something might be wrong, it recognises that unless leadership responds to appropriate challenges in the right way, no one is going to have the courage to say anything that deviates from what they believe to be the received view.[23]

Going further, creating an institutional expression to counter groupthink by supporting and encouraging "red teaming" is one of the ways to counter the effects of cognitive bias within a team.[24] Encouraging an attitude of open discussion and reasonable challenge throughout your command is also a healthy thing to do.[25] For example, one of the recommendations from the Op Telemeter report is that "loyalty to an 'oppo' is best expressed by challenging him before he makes a mistake rather than trying to cover up for him afterwards. Moreover, that encouraging someone to own up quickly to their mistakes is better than allowing them to hide them."[26]

Fostering critical thinking as an ongoing process can also help people avoid moral disengagement. Moral disengagement refers to the psychological manoeuvres that we use to engage in unethical behaviour while at the same time maintaining a positive self-concept—i.e., convincing ourselves that we've done nothing wrong.[27] We manage to do this by reinterpreting our actions so they seem less bad (e.g., who thinks of taking something they don't really need from the stationary cupboard as stealing), minimising our role or personal responsibility (e.g., "she told me to do it"), minimising or ignoring the consequences of our actions (e.g., "well it wasn't that bad"), or blaming and/or devaluing our victim (e.g., "well he deserved it").[28] The Op Telemeter report notes that "moral disengagement on the part of Sgt. Blackman and the members of his Multiple was a significant contributory factor in the handling and shooting of the insurgent."[29] Again, fostering an environment in which behaviours and attitudes are not just left unchallenged over time can help prevent this from developing.

Apply reward and discipline

"You get what you inspect" is part of leading by example. Whether formal or informal, inspections are a means by which you can communicate priorities. If things are overlooked, they quickly become invisible. Maintaining those standards, even in the face of adversity, is a function of effective leadership. This will be particularly challenging in "situations where 'the battle lines are not straight.' Training alone cannot mitigate these risks, strong leadership and regular oversight is required."[30]

If other people are doing it, it quickly becomes normal (think about speeding on the motorway and keeping up with traffic flow). Rules are important, and enforcing them is also important. In many contexts, simple rules applied consistently tend to outperform even expert judgment.[31] Therefore, rules matter. Do not let people start to see rules and laws as soft or "malleable," as this is dangerous and is often the start of a slippery slope. However, while rules are important, a heavy-handed approach to enforcing them can in some instances prove counterproductive. If minor infringements are treated in the same way as a major breaking of the rules, and every rule bending is treated as if it is a life and death matter when it comes to punishment, rather than prompting adherence to the rules, it can simply undermine the difference between things that don't really matter and things that are incredibly serious. If a punishment does not fit the crime, this can lead to people covering up for one another out of a sense of injustice at harsh punishment for trivial offences. Covering up undermines all of the rules, and the authority of those who make them. Therefore, each "crime" must be treated individually and in context, and the punishment must always fit the crime.[32]

Rewarding the behaviour you want to see is as, if not even more, important than applying discipline to prevent the behaviour you want to eliminate and will ultimately promote the behaviour you are seeking. These issues are just as true at the systemic level as they are at the individual one. As you move into positions to make decisions and set goals and standards that start affecting system-wide behaviours, understanding that there are likely to be unintended consequences is also important. A goal-orientated mentality can easily cause the narrowing of one's focus onto a specific point at the expense of noticing what else is happening as a result of one's actions. Organisations can be very effective at structuring individual actions into discrete parcels of activity (mostly unintentionally), so they do not necessarily see the outcomes or impacts of their decisions or actions at a later stage of the process they are involved with.[33] Getting out of your silo and gaining an appreciation of the effects of your orders is essential in determining if the new goals that you are implementing with the sweep of your pen are actually realistic for all the people they will affect. For example, a 2002 US Army War College report showed that army units had 297 days of annual mandatory training to pack into 256 available training days.[34] The message was clear—the system was obliging you to lie or face disciplinary measures. The result of such inappropriately set goals is that everybody lies, and everybody knows everybody else is lying. This will inevitably have a corrosive effect on other rules as well.

An organisation's ethical culture is degraded "when even good people feel they need to systematically falsify, fudge, and exaggerate in order to make the system work properly."[35] Creating the routine assumption that some rules are deliberately optional undermines the way other problems and situations are viewed, and there is the risk that people accustomed to making common sense exceptions to create good outcomes "start making lazy or corrupt exceptions to facilitate bad outcomes. Further, such a corrosive environment risks creating cynicism about the moral universe. Is all life just a game?"[36]

While you may not have responsibility for the whole system, you can and do have power to influence significant parts of it, so be aware what behaviour you are promoting through the goals that you set, especially the unintended ones.

Demand high performance

As a leader, you are in a position to shape group culture. While a leader can and should demand high standards, deliberately or accidentally creating an environment of fear where nobody is willing to admit to having done something wrong can not only be counterproductive, it can also be dangerous.[37] For example, Prof. Mike Skerker at USNA Annapolis recalls the case of a commodore who read the riot act over the fact that a new communications system was nonfunctional on several aircraft in his fleet. "During the next meeting, every subordinate reported to the commodore that the system on their crafts were 'green.' Great success, except that on some craft 'green' meant that communications could only be maintained for four minutes."[38] No one had lied, but they were too scared to tell the full truth, which in this case was rather important. Demanding perfection and making it clear that you will only accept zero defect reports is likely to prove counterproductive. For example, when it comes to dealing with allegations of sexual harassment, this type of thinking (and the signalling that goes with it) "can result in problems being improperly "contained" within the unit."[39] Given how difficult this kind of complaint is to make anyway, the added disincentive of upsetting an unblemished unit record, combined with the expectation that it won't be taken seriously anyway, means that "trust in already suspect complaint procedures erodes even further."[40] This suggests that sometimes, paradoxically, units that have zero reported sexual harassment incidents may be of more concern than other units that actually have reported cases; at least in the latter, people may feel empowered to report misconduct, meaning it can actually be addressed and dealt with.

Let people know what they do is important and that *you* as the leader value that work. The behavioural economist Dan Ariely notes that the meaningfulness of your work has a large part to play in how well you do it.[41] Your team will take those tasks more seriously as a result of your acknowledgement and be less tempted to cut corners. Cheating goes down when the stakes are higher, and thus work that is valued will be done to a higher standard than work that is not.

While setting inappropriate requirements can be damaging, being less than clear can also cause ethical issues. Ambiguity surrounding orders or expectations is a major cause of ethical failure. As already noted, fatigue is likely to be a factor on most deployments, and sleep restriction increases reliance on clear rules.[42] An absence of clear guidance is almost a guarantee for unintended outcomes. Being clear about what you value and what is expected in a given situation is essential and can have many profound effects for your team culture, the behaviour and mental health of your people. For example, during operations in Afghanistan in the first decade of the new millennium, personnel from many coalition states were repeatedly put in unenviable positions by their own governments who had instructed them to work with local populations and uphold their own values in doing so, but[43] in some areas, Thursday night was known as "man loving night." Had the activity been limited to consenting adults, then it would not have posed problems (indeed, many of the coalition states have legally recognised mar-riage between same-sex couples). However, these activities were of a very different nature. Checkpoints, supposedly set up to provide security to the local area, were instead being used as opportunities to target and select young prepubescent boys that "caught the local commander's eye." They would then be raped. At the time, this state of affairs was considered to be accepted practice by the indigenous coalition partner and could even occur in the outer cordon of the ISAF security perimeters occupied by those indigenous forces. Friday prayers were considered to absolve those involved of any sin. This put enormous pressure on personnel, many of whom requested guid-ance but received nothing and had little idea how to deal with a situation in which they were seemingly expected to go along with something that was wrong for policy reasons in order to keep the coalition together. [44]

In such situations, it is easy to see how ambiguity and uncertainty over the rules can also contribute to both post-traumatic stress disorder (PTSD) and moral injury. The term "moral injury" was proposed by the American psychologist Jonathan Shay a decade ago to describe unseen wounds thought to be distinct from the more closely studied experience of PTSD. Shay's definition, which remains widely quoted, suggests that moral injury is pres-ent when "there has been a betrayal of what is morally correct; by someone who holds legitimate authority; and, in a high-stakes situation."[45] Those who develop moral injuries are likely to experience negative thoughts about themselves or others (for example, "I am a terrible person" or "My bosses don't care about people's lives") as well as intense feelings of shame, guilt, or disgust. These symptoms can contribute to the development of mental health difficulties, including depression, post-traumatic stress disorder, and even suicidal ideation.[46]

Although there is a wealth of evidence that having a supportive "one up" protects your mental health, leaders are human too. As such, more senior leaders should keep an active eye on more junior ones and check how they are doing. If they show signs of presenteeism—insisting on carrying on with work despite being ill, injured, or unable to function at full capacity because of poor mental health—this will directly affect the operational capability and health of all team members, and thus early identification and support are key.[47] It was noted in Sgt. Blackman's Supreme Court Appeal that pastoral care had not been provided to the troops at Command Post Omar presumably due to it being too dangerous to be visited, and that Blackman (who had also not been trained in Trauma Risk Management (TRiM) pre-deployment) had no peer support network.[48] This left Blackman and his immediate team badly at risk.[49]

Given the stigma associated with seeking help, it is often difficult for people to ask for it, meaning it is up to leaders to recognise and address this. Supporting those who may not wish to be supported is also important, especially those who might be "too busy," as avoidance is a key symptom of trauma.[50] To date, the language used to describe moral injury has lacked precision, which has contributed to the difficulties associated with differentiating moral injury from PTSD. As such, moral injury is often considered as a "mental health issue" rather than an unavoidable feature of uniformed service that needs to be managed by commanders at all levels.[51]

Encourage confidence in the team

Recognising team members as people and understanding you are not just a leader but also a part of that team is important in preventing an accidental drift into acquiring the traits of toxic leadership.[52] Just as the role of the leader is vitally important in shaping both expectations and the ethical climate of the group,[53] the group itself is also a significant actor in its own right, and peer-to-peer influence is a powerful factor.[54] Appreciating the role of the group itself is therefore an essential part of ethical leadership,[55] as is appreciating the fact that the support of ethical norms by immediate peers and direct leaders is even more influential than that of senior military officers.[56]

There is a significant body of research demonstrating that group identity can have a profound impact on behaviour, both good and bad. If the group has a strong positive identity, that is itself an excellent defence against ethical drift, while if you see other members of the group breaking rules or cheating, it spreads further very fast.[57] Group identity prompts people to ask, "What do *we* do in this situation?" If you see fellow group members breaking the rules or cheating, then the chances are you will too, whereas seeing other people passing up "opportunities" or doing the right thing, that too will tend to get mirrored.[58]

It is about more than simply following the legal rules. The International Committee of the Red Cross report Roots of Restraint, published in 2018, recognised that culture is an essential part of understanding why people don't break the rules—simply focusing on the rules alone would be less successful than also appreciating and nurturing an ethical culture in the organisation.[59] Group behaviour is contagious—we like to conform to the social environment around us. That is one of the reasons that situations in which our individual identity can be hidden from the group are more likely to lead to bad behaviour. So, for example, concealing one's identity—even something as simple as covering one's face—can have a powerful impact on people's ethical behaviour. People can lose their self-awareness and feel less accountable for their actions. This "deindividuation" has been found to increase people's willingness to harm others unnecessarily.[60] Anthropological research has found that cultures that cover their faces (e.g., using face paint or masks) during combat were more likely to kill, torture, and mutilate their enemy than cultures that did not cover their faces.[61]

Trust is an enormous part of having confidence in your team. Operational demands can make it hard to maintain the group cohesion of shared understanding and expectation that builds that trust. For example, unit disaggregation is particularly common among Special Operations Forces personnel who are regularly tasked to support short-duration missions that are distinct and separate from their unit's regular tasking.[62] This can contribute to the slow erosion of leadership, discipline, and accountability. These risks should be recognised, and opportunities should be seized to reinforce a healthy group ethos.

Multiagency, multinational, or complex situations can also pose challenges for trust. "Establishing trust within, and between, groups from different organisations or cultural backgrounds is an essential prerequisite to effective partnering."[63] On the other side of the coin, while healthy competition between units is to be expected, if your team starts to see itself as separate, or "better" than those other groups, it can not only undermine wider trust, it can easily slip into dangerous exceptionalism. Subgroups within militaries that have a strong identity—i.e., groups that see themselves as unique and distinct from the rest of the military—have contributed to unethical behaviour in the past. For example, the disgraced Canadian Airborne Regiment that was disbanded following the crimes committed by some of its members in Somalia, had developed an exceptionalism that was so extreme, they wouldn't even salute officers that were outside their regiment.[64] Using language that differentiates between "us" and "them" can also contribute to unhealthy attitudes because "they" are not considered the same as "us." For example, there is clear evidence that in war, incidents of war crimes are far higher when a conflict is deemed to be racialised.[65] This logic extends beyond that particular environment and there should always be zero tolerance for derogatory speech due to its corrosive influence on perceptions and behaviour.

Recognise individual strengths and weaknesses

As has already been mentioned above, character is very important to the military, from recruitment and development all the way through to promotion. It is understood to be a stable set of behavioural dispositions, formed by habit and education, which can supposedly be relied upon to guide individuals' actions and which others can use as a relatively reliable basis for predicting their behaviour.[66] We judge people based on the type of character they appear to possess, and this informs our expectations about whether or not they are trustworthy, honest, will have the courage to speak out when something is wrong, whether they will be diligent and contentious even when not being supervised. But is this really safe? Moral failure, ethical transgression, and law breaking are often seen as character failures as a result, even though we have already seen just how important situational factors can be in affecting people's behaviour and perceptions. Lack of sleep can have a profound effect on the ethical awareness of individuals, and it can also cause individual behaviour to vary dramatically. Character may have an influence on this, but it is not enough to fully protect people from this or many other situational factors. This is just as true of leaders as it is subordinates. The Op Telemeter Internal Review points to the fact that environment can have a profound effect on maintaining rules and regulations, but that current training appears lacking in terms of appreciating this.[67] Therefore, to build on strengths and minimise weaknesses, leaders at all levels of an organisation should promote ethical and prosocial behaviour through ethics training and mentoring.[68]

"Train as you intend to fight" is not limited to weapons drill and tactics. Situation and context can have powerful effects on perception and action, but this is something that should be taken into account when considering how best to go about it. That means that to foster genuine ethical resilience, you need to go beyond knowing what the right thing to do is and get people to actually do it even when it is hard. Fostering ethical behaviour has to extend beyond dialogue, moral reasoning, the consideration of stated institutional values, and other deliberative processing. Because people's best intentions can be overridden by situational factors, ethics training and education need to include strategies that actually influence behaviour. To do this, you need approaches that tap into automatic thought processes or that help people to switch from deliberative to automatic processing.[69] So, when it comes to applying what you know, the closer you can get in training to the actual environment you are training for, the better. That means that best practice needs to embrace a full range of learning environments. Messervey gives us some illustrations of what this might look like:

> First, ethics training can be conducted in a non-stressful environment so that key lessons can be absorbed (such as the impact that crowds can have on ethical decision making). This information can be repeated to increase retention of key lessons. Next, ethics training can simulate stressful situations (such as surprise and shock) to teach soldiers how to respond when confronted with ethical dilemmas under stressful conditions. This can also allow soldiers to practise coping with strong emotions such as anger. Finally, when conducting scenario-based training, soldiers and leaders can practice intervening during a staged ethical misconduct.[70]

If you can normalise the discussion of ethical issues rather than treat it as something separate from routine activities, this can have a constant affirmation of what you are trying to promote, whether you are in a formal training environment or in an informal moment between other tasks.[71]

Invariably, there is never enough time available to do everything you want to. Sometimes, that time is incredibly restricted due to factors out of anyone's control. That is why it is so important not to leave this essential area until just before a deployment. It should be a normal part of everyday activity. As long as it is not considered simply as an afterthought, and is therefore part of routine activity, it is relatively easy to focus on a particular area that might need to be refreshed, such as judgmental scenarios based on expected situations just before a unit is deployed, rather than having to start from scratch just when there is no time to do it properly.

Given the fact that it is always possible to do more, how much military ethics training or education is sufficient? A definitive answer is not possible, but we do know that even short courses, delivered in the right way, by the right people, using the right material and methods of delivery can have very real results on the behaviour of personnel deployed on operations.[72] Just reminding people about good behaviour makes them behave better.[73] For example, a training package, delivered to a US Infantry Brigade, based on movie vignettes and leader-led discussions, was administered seven to eight months into a fifteen-month high-intensity combat deployment in Iraq, between December 11, 2007, and January 30, 2008. Reports of unethical behaviour and attitudes in this group were compared with a randomly selected sample from the same brigade, pre-training. The ethics intervention, limited though it was, was associated with significantly lower rates of unethical conduct of soldiers and a greater willingness to report and address misconduct than in those before training or for those that did not receive it.[74] Imagine what a more robust approach to ethics education might achieve in building strength and reducing weaknesses in team behaviours.

Strive for team goals

We have seen how important identifying with other people can be and how this influences behaviour, both good and bad. If we are surrounded by people doing the right thing, that tends to rub off. We have also seen how people do a better job and cut fewer corners if they believe their work is important, and therefore, how important it is for leaders to set clear team goals and demonstrate an appreciation of each individual's role in pursuing them.

Group goals are one of the factors influencing the creation of a shared identity. They don't necessarily replace individual goals, but exist along-side them, although certain situations may bring them to the fore. "For example on a combat patrol the group identity would be more salient, and as such collective goals will take precedent over personal ones... This can have tragic consequences for the individual, when a soldier throws himself on a grenade to save his buddies."[75] This kind of extreme self-sacrifice to save the group is motivated by a "visceral sense of oneness with the group, resulting from intense collective experiences."[76] However, the type of routine, smaller sacrifices that members of a team make for each other in pursuit of a shared goal are also important.[77] This has many implications, one of which being that if people are prepared to "pull their weight" and demonstrate a shared commitment to a common goal or task, they can be accepted by the group even if they are not liked by other members of it. For example, in Sebastian Junger's account of US soldiers in Afghanistan, Sgt. O'Byrne states: "there are guys in the platoon who straight up hate each other [...] but they would also die for each other."[78]

There is also evidence of a relationship between unit-cohesion and mental health outcomes in soldiers. Membership of a group can "provide meaning to life, encourage the provision and receipt of social support, facilitate social influence, and engender a sense of belongingness."[79] This sense of connection to those "who share our sense of self and the group itself" can enhance well-being, in terms of mental and physical health.[80]

Team goals are clearly an important motivator and can help forge a common sense of identity that is an essential part of creating a healthy ethical culture within an organisation. However, there is also one more significant factor that must be guarded against. We have already looked at the dangers of groupthink, but a related, and just as dangerous, tendency within groups with a clear goal and a sense of righteousness is moral certainty. Given how much time we spend convincing ourselves that we are on the right side, that our cause is just and that we have sufficient legitimacy to permit us to do what needs to be done, it may seem strange to warn against being too confident in your goals. However, Steve Reicher at the University of St. Andrews makes a powerful argument that the biggest harms can be done by people who *really* believe they are doing the right thing. Reicher reexamined a number of supposedly well-known psychological experiments and, in light of new notes and evidence that had emerged since, found that the "received view" of why people had acted in the way they had may not be safe at all. For example, the longstanding conclusion from Milgram's experiments in 1961 was that normal people will tend to be obedient to authority figures even if that means applying lethal levels of electric shock to subjects who have gotten a maths problem wrong. Similarly, the conclusion that we have taken for many years from Zimbardo's Stanford Prison Experiment in 1971 is that people are predisposed to conform to roles, and guard brutality was a natural consequence of people "asserting the power inherent in that role."[81] Reicher's reexamination suggests something else had been missed—and that this was at least, if not more important than the explanations that we have been used to.

While other factors were undoubtedly also at play, one of the reasons that the subjects in Milgram's experiment were content to electrocute someone, or Zimbardo's guards were motivated to abuse inmates to impose discipline in a fantasy prison, may have been because they believed they were contributing to science that would ultimately help humankind. Both groups had been primed to look at the "big picture" (for example, helping future generations of children to learn more effectively, or reducing prison violence through reform) and this goal meant that individuals rationalised that the immediate harm they were inflicting was not as important as the worthy goal that was being pursued.[82]

Such behaviour can be observed in many areas of life. For example, in British justice, disclosure of unused evidence to the other side is an essential part of a police investigation and ensuing prosecution through the courts. This is to ensure that important leads really are followed up and miscarriages of justice can be avoided (e.g., when it turns out the person had an alibi all along). A failure to disclose awkward or conflicting evidence by the police is therefore a serious matter, but it is far more likely to occur if the investigating officer is certain that they have caught the right person. The trial process in which evidence is tested to see if it stands up to scrutiny can be seen as rather inconvenient "red tape" if the problem has clearly already been solved as far as the officer is concerned.[83] Therefore, it is easy to see how if someone is confident that they've got the right person, they are more likely to bend the rules a little to ensure that nothing gets in the way of successfully holding them to account.[84]

It is easy to see how on a larger-scale, moral certainty leads to crusades where anything appears to be justified in the pursuit of "the good." An otherwise good person doing the wrong thing because they believe in a goal can be just as dangerous as a bad person deliberately causing harm. Therefore, getting the balance right between inspiring the confidence in your team that they are doing the right thing without giving them the misplaced belief that therefore anything goes in pursuing that goal is one of the hardest challenges that leaders need to consider.

Conclusion

While such a short piece cannot hope to be comprehensive, this paper has employed the headings from the Army Leadership Code to draw out key points related to both how things can go wrong, and what you can do to ensure that this doesn't happen on your watch. Ethical leadership is simply part of good leadership. As such, it requires "focus, the appropriate use of resources, trust, effective decision making, and provision of model behaviour that is worth following." It is also therefore true that "once it is lost it is difficult if not impossible to regain"[85] While ensuring your organisation has an ethical climate is unlikely to win you a conflict, poor or absent ethics can hamper or contribute to ethical failings that undermine or lose war efforts.[86]

Notes

1. The author would like to gratefully acknowledge the generous assistance provided by Dr. Deanna Messervey, Department of National Defence, Ottawa, Canada, and insights from Messervey, D. L. (2020). *Ethical Risk Checklist*. Director General Military Personnel Research and Analysis Scientific Report. Ottawa, ON, Canada.
2. O'Keefe, D., Messervey, D., and Squires, E., (2018). Promoting Ethical and Prosocial Behavior: The Combined Effect of Ethical Leadership and Coworker Ethicality. *Ethics and Behavior*, 28(3), 235.
3. Army Leadership Code (2015) 1st Edition, Centre for Army Leadership. https://www.army.mod.uk/media/2698/ac72021_the_army_leadership_code_an_introductory_guide.pdf.
4. For example, the Op Telemeter Internal Review into the circumstances surrounding the "murder of an unknown insurgent in…Helmand Province, Afghanistan on 15th Sep 11 by Sgt Blackman." The redacted Executive Summary notes that the deployment "provides a number of important lessons on creating an appropriate command culture in a complex environment; both the pitfalls and examples of best practice. These should be used to inform future commanders and those they lead in order to reduce the likelihood of a repetition of the sort of behaviour exhibited by Sgt Blackman and his multiple." Executive Summary, Op Telemeter Internal Report. Annex B-2 to NCHQ/585/5, 2 Jul15. It therefore sincerely hoped that the full, unredacted report will eventually be released so that those lessons can indeed be learnt.
5. D. Whetham (2009). 'The Moral, Legal and Ethical Dimensions of War at the Joint Services Command and Staff College', in Robinson, Connolly, and Carrick (Eds), *Ethics Education for Irregular Warfare* (Ashgate).
6. Michael Skerker, David Whetham, and Don Carrick (Eds) (2019). *Military Virtues: Practical Guidance for Service Personnel at Every Career Stage* (Howgate Press).
7. Ibid. While there is insufficient space to explore the difference between values and virtues here, Skerker, Whetham and Carrick explore this in some depth.
8. Lammers, J., Galinsky, A., Dubois, D., and Rucker D., (2015). Power and Morality. *Current Opinion in Psychology*, 6, pp.15-19. See also Lammers, J., Stoker, J. I., Jordan, J., Pollmann, M., and Stapel, D. A. (2011). Power increases infidelity among men and women. *Psychological science*, 22(9), 1191–1197.
9. Dean C. Ludwig & Clinton O. Longenecker (1993). The Bathsheba Syndrome: The Ethical Failure of Successful Leaders. *Journal of Business Ethics*. 12, 265-273.
10. Christopher M. Barnes (2018). Sleep Well, Lead Better. *Harvard Business Review*, Sep-Oct. https://hbr.org/2018/09/sleep-well-lead-better.
11. C. Barnes, J. Schaubroeck, M. Huth, S. Ghumman (2011). Lack of Sleep and Unethical Conduct. *Organizational Behavior and Human Decision Processes*. 115(2), 169-180.
12. R. P. Larsen (2001). Decision Making by Military Students Under Severe Stress. *Military Psychology*. Vol 13, Issue 2, 89–98.
13. H. Dai, K. L. Milkman, D. A. Hofmann, B. R. Staats (2014). The Impact of Time at Work and Time Off From Work on Rule Compliance: The Case of Hand Hygiene in Healthcare. *The Wharton School Research Paper* No.56.
14. M. Kouchaki and I. Smith (2014), The Morning Morality Effect: The Influence of Time of Day on (Un)ethical Behavior. *Psychological Science*. 24, 95–102.
15. Christopher M. Barnes (2018). Sleep Well, Lead Better. *Harvard Business Review*, Sep-Oct. https://hbr.org/2018/09/sleep-well-lead-better.
16. Leaders can also affect an organisation's tone when it comes to the stigma of mental health. See Tom McDermott (2017). "We Need To Talk About Marine A": Constant War, Diminished Responsibility and the Case of Alexander Blackman. *Australian Centre for the Study of Armed Conflict and Society. Occasional paper Series* No. 6.
17. Sandy Woodward (1992). *One Hundred Days: The Memoirs of the Falklands Battle Group Commander* (London: HarperCollins Publishers), 103–104.

18. Understanding and decision making (2010, updated 2016), JDP 04 2nd Edition, p.39. https://www.gov.uk/government/publications/jdp-04-understanding
19. https://metro.co.uk/2019/10/02/man-drove-van-fast-flowing-river-sat-nav-told-10851190/.
20. JDP 04 2nd Edition, p.41
21. JDP 04 2nd Edition, p.25
22. https://webarchive.nationalarchives.gov.uk/20171123122743/http://www.iraqinquiry.org.uk/the-report/.
23 https://assets.publishing.service.gov.uk/government/uploads/system/uploads/attachment_data/file/674545/TheGoodOperation_WEB.PDF. Specifically note p.62—Embracing Challenge.
24. JDP 04 2nd Edition, p.52.
25. Muel Kaptein (1998). Ethics Management. *Issues in Business Ethics*, vol 10. (Springer) 31–45; Muel Kaptein (2008). Developing and Testing a Measure for the Ethical Culture of Organizations: The Corporate Ethical Virtues Model. *Journal of Organizational Behaviour.* Vol. 29. Issue 7, 923–947.
26. Recommendations, *Op Telemeter Internal Report.* Annex C-1 to NCHQ/585/5, 2 Jul15
27. A. Bandura (1999). Moral Disengagement in the Perpetration of Inhumanities. *Personality and Social Psychology Review.* Vol 3. Issue 3. 193–209.
28. Ibid.
29. Executive Summary, *Op Telemeter Internal Report*. Annex B-2 to NCHQ/585/5, 2 Jul15.
30. Recommendations, *Op Telemeter Internal Report.* Annex C-1 to NCHQ/585/5, 2 Jul15.
31. M. A. Bishop and J. D. Trout (2002) 50 years of successful predictive modelling should be enough: Lessons for philosophy of science. *Philosophy of Science.* 69, 197–208.
32. C. Ostwind and C. Dunlap (1999). The Honor Concept of the US Naval Academy http://isme.tamu.edu/JSCOPE99/Navy99.html.
33. Adams and Balfour, *Unmasking Administrative Evil* (Routledge: 2015).
34. Leonard Wong (2002). *Stifling Innovation: Developing Tomorrow's Leaders Today*, Carlisle, PA: Strategic Studies Institute, U.S. Army War College.
35. Michael Skerker, 'Honesty', in Skerker, Whetham and Carrick, *Military Virtues.*
36. Ibid.
37. It may have been this kind of fear that led to the Captain of a guided-missile destroyer to be removed from command for filing false reports about his ship's position rather than admit that a technical problem meant the ship was dead in the water. https://www.sandiegouniontribune.com/news/military/story/2020-04-12/navy-destroyer-captain-relieved-in-january-after-lying-to-san-diego-fleet-command-about-ships-position.
38. Michael Skerker, 'Honesty', in Skerker, Whetham and Carrick, *Military Virtues.*
39. The Secretary of the Army's Senior Review Panel Report on Sexual Harassment: Volume 1 (1997), DIANE Publishing, p.48
40. Ibid.
41. Dan Ariely (2012). *What Makes Us Feel Good About Our Work?* https://www.ted.com/talks/dan_ariely_what_makes_us_feel_good_about_our_work.
42. O. K. Olsen, S. Pallesen, J. Eid (2010). The Impact of Partial Sleep Deprivation on Moral Reasoning in Military Officers. *Sleep* 33 (8), 1086–90.
43. This case study is taken from David Whetham (2017). ABCA Coalition Operations in Afghanistan, Iraq and Beyond: Two Decades of Military Ethics Challenges and Leadership Responses, in Olsthoorn, P. (ed.), *Military Ethics and Leadership* (Brill Nijhoff, International Studies in Military Ethics; vol. 3)
44. Whetham, D., Interviews with ABCA personnel (conducted May–July 2009). In Whetham, *Coalition Operations.*
45. Jonathan Shay (1995). *Achilles in Vietnam.* Pocket Books.
46. Greenberg N, Docherty M, Gnanapragasam S, Wessely S. (2020). Managing mental health challenges faced by healthcare workers during covid-19 pandemic, *British Medical Journal*; 368 :m1211 DOI: https://doi.org/10.1136/bmj.m1211.

47. Jones N, Seddon R, Fear NT, McAllister P, Wessely S, Greenberg N. (2012). Leadership, cohesion, morale, and the mental health of UK armed forces in Afghanistan. *Psychiatry.* 75, 49–59. doi:10.1521/psyc.2012.75.1.49 pmid:22397541.

48. N. Greenberg, V. Langston and N. Jones (2008). Trauma Risk Management (TRiM) in the UK Armed Forces. *Journal of the Roayal Army Medical Corps.* 154(2), 124–7.

49. *Regina v Alexander Blackman* (2017) 190 EWCA para 99 (ii).

50. Greenberg N., Thomas S., Iversen A., Unwin C., Hull L., Wessely S. (2003). Who do military peacekeepers want to talk about their experiences? Perceived psychological support of UK military peacekeepers on return from deployment. *Journal of Mental Health.* 12:565-73. doi:10.1080/09638230310001627928

51. Where moral injury is not coincident with PTSD it should be considered an existential condition needing to be addressed rather than being deemed a disorder that ought to be treated. See Tom Frame (2015). *Moral Injury: Unseen Wounds in an Age of Barbarism.* UNSW Press.

52. Everyone knows that toxic leaders use their subordinates, but it is the power inherent in their position that makes this possible. Power increases the objectification and stereotyping of others. This means that those in positions of power are more likely to see others in terms of their usefulness in obtaining their own goals. Moreover, while people in positions of low power, unsurprisingly, tend to pay attention to those in power, this is not reciprocated. Those with power tend to pay less attention to the needs of those they have control over. See D. H. Gruenfeld, M. E. Inesi, J. C. Magee, A. D. Galinsky (2008). Power and Objectification of Social Targets. *Journal of Personality and Social Psychology.* 95(1), 111–27; S. T. Fiske (1993). Controlling Other People: The Impact of Power on Stereotyping. *American Psychologist.* 48(6), 621–628.

53. Schminke, M., Ambrose, M. L., and Neubaum, D. O. (2005). The effect of leader moral development on ethical climate and employee attitudes. *Organizational Behavior and Human Decision Processes*, 97(2), 135–151.

54. O'Keefe, Messervey, and Squires (2018) *op.cit.* suggest that understanding the relationship between these two groups is important.

55. D. M. Mayer, S. Nurmohamed, L. K. Treviño, D. L. Shapiro, and M. Schminke (2013). Encouraging Employees to Report Unethical Conduct Internally: It Takes a Village. *Organizational Behavior and Human Decision Processes* 121. 89–103; O'Keefe, Messervey, and Squires (2018), *op cit.*

56. M. Murdoch, J. B. Pryor, M. A. Polusny, G. D. Gackstetter, and D. Cowper Ripley (2009). Local Social Norms and Military Sexual Stressors: Do Senior Officers' Norms Matter? *Military Medicine* 174 (10), 1100–4; see also G. R. Weaver, L. K.. Treviño, and B. Agle (2005). "Somebody I Look Up To:" Ethical Role Models in Organizations. *Organizational Dynamics.* 34(4), 313–330.

57. Unethical behaviour by peers is often judged less harshly than those outside of the group. F. Gino and A. D. Galinsky (2012). Vicarious Dishonesty: When Psychological Closeness Creates Distance from One's Moral Compass. *Organizational Behavior and Human Decision Processes.* 119, 15–26.

58. Dan Ariely (2013). *The Honest Truth About Dishonesty: How We Lie to Everyone—Especially Ourselves* (New York), 197–207.

59. International Committee of the Red Cross (2018), *The Roots of Restraint in War* https://www.icrc.org/en/publication/roots-restraint-war.

60. S. Bochner ed. (1982). Cultures in Contact: Studies in Cross Cultural Interaction (Pergamon Press); A. Silke ed.(2003). *Psychological Perspectives on Terrorism and Its Consequences* (John Wiley and Sons); P. G. Zimbardo (1969). 'The Human Choice: Individuation, Reason, and Order Versus Deindividuation, Impulse and Chaos.' In W. J. Arnold and D. Levine (eds), *Nebraska Symposium on Motivation.* (University of Nebraska Press).

61. R. I. Watson (1973). Investigation into Deindividuation Using a Cross Cultural Survey Technique. *Journal of Personality and Psychology.* 25, 342–345.

62. USSOCOM Comprehensive Review Report, 2020. p. 31.

63. JDP 04 2nd Edition, p.53

64. D. Winslow (1997). *The Canadian Airborne Regiment in Somalia; A Socio-Cultural Inquiry.* (Minister of Public works and Government Services, Canada).

65. J. W. Dower (1986). *War Without Mercy: Race and Power in the Pacific War* (Pantheon Books).

66. Martin L. Cook (2015), 'Military Ethics and Character Development,' in George R. Lucas (Ed.), *Routledge Handbook of Military Ethics* (Routledge), p.98

67. Recommendations, *Op Telemeter Internal Report.* Annex C-1 to NCHQ/585/5, 2 Jul15

68. Robinson, P., de Lee, N. and Carrick, D. (eds), *Ethics Education in the Military* (Ashgate 2008).

69. D. L. Messervey (2013). What drives moral attitudes and behaviour? *Director General Military Personnel Research and Analysis Technical Report TR 2013-003* (Ottawa: Defence Research and Development, Canada).

70. D. Messervey and J. M. Peach (2014). Battlefield Ethics: What Infuences Ethical Behaviour on Operations? In *The Human Dimensions of Operations: A Personal Research Perspective* (Canadian Defence Academy Press).

71. One of the ways this can be done is using the King's Centre for Military Ethics Education Playing Cards—a non-threatening and accessible way to raise ethical questions, with QR web links to guidance and support to help people reach the most appropriate answers: https://militaryethics.uk/en/playing-cards/military

72. Warner, Appenzeller, Mobbs, Parker, Warner, Grieger, and Hoge (2010) "Effectiveness of battlefield-ethics training during combat deployment: a programme assessment", *Lancet* 378: 915-24.

73. Ariely found that even reminding people of non-existent rules is enough to make them behave better. N. Mazar, O. Amir, D. Ariely (2008). The Dishonesty of Honest People: A Theory of Self-Concept Maintenance. *Journal of Marketing Research.* Vol. XLV, 633–644.

74. Warner et al. *Battlefield-ethics training.*

75. S. Schilling, *Cohesion in Modern Military Formations* (King's College London, unpublished thesis 2019)

76. Harvey Whitehouse (2018) Dying for the group: Towards a general theory of extreme self-sacrifice. *Behavioral and Brain Sciences.* Vol 41, e192.

77. The task cohesion (a commitment to work together as a coordinated entity in the pursuit of common goals) and social cohesion (when defined as a common identity around a shared sense of attraction) are overlapping and mutually enforcing. See S. Schilling, *Cohesion in Modern Military Formations* (King's College London, unpublished thesis 2019).

78. S. Junger (2010). War. (Twelve), 79. Quoted in S. Schilling, *Cohesion in Modern Military Formations* (King's College London, unpublished thesis 2019).

79. T. Cruwys, S. A. Haslam, G. A. Dingle, C. Haslam, J. Jetten (2014). Depression and Social Identity: An Integrative Review. *Personality and Social Psychology Review.* 18(3), 215–238: 228–229.

80. S. A. Haslam, S. Reicher (2007). Identity Entrepreneurship and the Consequences of Identity Failure: The Dynamics of Leadership in the BBC Prison Study. *Social Psychology Quarterly.* 70, 125–147.

81. S. Reicher, A. Haslam, and J. Van Bavel (2019) How the Stanford Prison Experiment Gave Us the Wrong Idea About Evil, *Prospect*, March. https://www.prospectmagazine.co.uk/magazine/how-the-stanford-prison-experiment-gave-us-the-wrong-ideal-about-evil.

82. Ibid. See also: S. Reicher, A. Haslam, and J. Van Bavel (2019). Rethinking the Nature of Cruelty: The Role of Identity Leadership in the Stanford Prison Experiment. *American Psychologist.* Aug. https://doi.org/10.1037/amp0000443.

83. Psychologists use the term "hypothesis confirmation" to refer to looking for evidence that supports your view and failing to look for evidence that disconfirms your hypothesis.

84. Anon (2019). The Secret Barrister: Stories of the Law and How It's Broken (Picador), chs. 8 and 9.

85. Dean Ludwig and Clinton O. Longenecker (1993). The Bathsheba Syndrome: The Ethical Failure of Successful Leaders. *Journal of Business Ethics* 12, 272.

86. D. Whetham (2015). 'Expeditionary Ethics Education,' in George R. Lucas, *Routledge Handbook of Military Ethics* (Routledge).

Where is the Justice?
What We Don't Know about Cyber Ethics*

Jennifer Petrie-Wyman

Anthony Rodi

Richard Albert McConnell

Introduction

Due to the pandemic and the rapidly changing cyber situation that society finds itself in today, every walk of life is finding ways to employ Internet solutions to whatever discipline in which they are trying to operate to support social distancing and flattening the curve. In times like this people may hurriedly seek solutions without considering the ethical ramifications. Twitter and Facebook have revolutionized social connection through cyber innovation. Yet the year of 2020 revealed the unanticipated consequences of the misapplication of open-source free- speech cyber platforms. What happens when cyber innovations are misapplied to misinformation campaigns and leveraged to support hate speech and violence? Do we have the right to lie to others in the cyber domain? Should Twitter and Facebook be permitted to de-platform bad actors? Most might agree that we should prevent bad actors in the cyber domain from inciting violence and criminal activity, but we may not understand the specific ramifications of the cyber environment in which these actions are operating. How do we begin to educate citizens on cyber misinformation, virtual hate speech, and ultimately each citizen's role in fostering ethics in the cyber domain?

Data and how it is managed is becoming increasingly important in this rapidly evolving situation in the cyberspace that may have far reaching consequences to society (White et al., 2019). For example, should an educator conducting a virtual class over the Internet record that class session? Many might say, Why not? Would their answer change if they discovered that

---

* Note: This article is a shortened version of a conference paper presented in March 2021.

that video recording was backed up on the cloud indefinitely (*Collaborate Ultra—File and Recording Storage FAQ, Behind the Blackboard!*, 2020)? Is it possible that such videos could compromise personally identifiable information (PII) and thus violate the Family Educational Rights and Privacy Act (FERPA) (Hlavac & Easterly, 2015)? If that teacher deletes that recording out of the classroom, is it deleted from the cloud, or does that data become orphaned data? If so, what are the ramifications of orphan data (Shepley, 2016)? What societal problems could result with a lack of trust in our digital systems? What systems, policies, and procedures are we putting into place to prevent damage to digital trust in our society (Lynch et al., 2016)? When capturing and storing data, are we really getting informed consent from those who provide the data when most informed consents are so confusing and often not read, and if read, not understood (Thomson, 2019; Petroni et al., 2016)? Should access to cyber education be limited to those with the highest aptitude or the most money, or do all citizens necessitate foundational cyber knowledge? Policy and lawmakers should grapple with questions like these. Such questions might have been useful in the increasingly less-fictional case of *Jurassic Park* regarding the ethical ramifications of introducing dinosaurs into the modern world (Spielberg, 1993). The above questions indicate there is a gap in the body of knowledge regarding cyber ethics and how data is curated. One of our problems in understanding this gap in knowledge is a lack of ability to understand how we got to this point.

One need only look at the current pandemic to see inequalities in education based on household access to the Internet. The Internet is a system of systems with an economic culture that is complex and potentially confusing for average users (Greenstein, 2020). The reality of inequalities, in terms of access combined with considerable sums of money, could create an environment fertile for unethical behavior to spawn. On the one hand, some might claim there are standards and accepted practices in cyber that would encourage ethical practice; they just need to be enforced in some meaningful way (Brantly, 2016). On the other hand, the Internet continues to evolve in some ways like ungoverned spaces and could cause some to ponder the need for improved programs for studying cyber ethics. Either way, researchers and practitioners should investigate how to apply ethics in this complex environment.

Therefore, the above-discussed Internet realities might suggest the need to address the following problem: The problem encouraging unethical behavior in cyberspace is Perceived Cognitive Distance (PCD), a culture of rationalization that excuses bad acts over cyberspace, a lack of individual and collective accountability, and a lack of cohesive policies governing data curation. New programs promoting ethics education tailored to the unique complexities of cyberspace could potentially address the above problem statement. A new model of cyber ethics leadership may also provide structural solutions to this problem.

The Current Cyber Ethics Leadership Gap

In 2021, it will be thirty years since the world wide web became publicly accessible. This cyber revolution triggered large-scale transformations across computer science, communication, social and political structures, economic functions, and individual behaviors (Berners-Lee & Fischetti, 2000). While the world has witnessed tremendous growth in the speed, application, and access to cyber technologies, only over the past ten years have scientists and professionals started to critically examine the outcomes and impact of the cyber use from an empirical perspective on a broad scale (Silfversten et al., 2019a; Yaghmaei et al., 2020a). The concept and function of cyber ethics, cyber ethics education, and cyber ethics leadership has just started to gain momentum across industry experts, policy analysts, educators, and citizen cyber users (Silfversten et al., 2019b; Yaghmaei et al., 2020b).

The COVID-19 global pandemic has further propelled the field of cyber ethics as businesses, organizations, institutions, and schools are quickly adapting to working in a fully virtual world. This virtual waterfall has exposed both our nation's cyber readiness as well as our cyber vulnerabilities, including a deficit in cyber ethics training and inequities in access to cyber technologies (Craig, 2019; Lee, 2019; Yaghmaei et al., 2020b). The Black Lives Matter Movement of 2020 has further unearthed a deficit in cyber leadership rooted in ethics and justice as businesses and tech firms have had to confront their own systemic racism and sexism. This article aims to build synergy on the significance and impact of cyber ethics across sectors, propose a broad-scale leadership change model, and formulate policy recommendations to advance cyber ethics education and leadership in the US with potential application to other countries.

The growing concern for cyber ethics has also accelerated due to an explosion in large- scale cyberattacks, data breaches, and the rise of nation-state hackers interfering with elections and government agencies. The field of cybersecurity has started to incorporate cyber ethics, yet significant gaps in the quality and quantity of cyber ethics training remain across industry, the military, and the education sector. The shortcomings of current cyber ethics educational programs are compounded by the fact the US is confronting a cybersecurity and tech workforce deficit, in which there is a pipeline shortage of qualified job applicants with requisite skills to work in jobs related to cyber defense (*K12 Computer Science Framework*, 2016a). The US is also confronting a shortage of teachers capable of teaching computer science education and the skills necessary to effectively instruct cyber education and cyber ethics education on a broad scale (Gross, 2018; *K12 Computer Science Framework*, 2016b).

The PCD of the cyber domain provides ripe ground for unethical cyber actions. At the same time, this PCD has also perpetuated an insulated tech sector often blind to the inequities in its own workforce. The professional computer science and cybersecurity workforce is disproportionately composed of white males and Asian American males (*K12 Computer Science Framework*, 2016b; Martin et al., 2015). This article examines cyber ethics as fundamentally interconnected to inclusion, equity, and justice.

Recent research findings are yielding significant insights into the need to reconsider and expand our knowledge and application of cyber ethics across multiple sectors (Yaghmaei et al., 2020b). The call to integrate cyber ethics into education and training across sectors is emerging in order to promote digital citizenship, national and global security, democracy, and racial and social justice (Mossberger et al., 2008; Yaghmaei et al., 2020b). Cyber ethics can transform professions and society to be more conscious of cyber threats, privacy, and inequities, which would then encourage the development of cyber solutions that promote justice, equity, and democratic rights.

The Elephant in the Cyber Ethics Room: Cyber Privilege, Inequity, and Justice

From the foundation of computing, inequity has persisted in the cyber workforce. The cyber and Internet revolution promised to democratize our world, creating an interactive global audience, reducing barriers to press and entrepreneurship success, yet the gains of cyber have often benefited a limited group of people, largely white male professionals from middle to high-income backgrounds. In 2015, only 24.7% of those employed in computer and mathematical occupations were female, 8.6% Black or African American, and 6.8% Hispanic or Latino (Greening, 2012; *K12 Computer Science Framework*, 2016b). Similar trends can be observed across gender and historically marginalized populations globally, with white males comprising 92% of the tech developer profession and professionals with white or European descent making up 72% of developers (Kapor Center, 2021; StackOverflow, 2019). Recent tech professionals are beginning to call out this inequity not only in the workforce, but in the design of the technology referring to cyber racial injustice as the "New Jim Code" (Benjamin, 2019). While corporations and higher education institutions are attempting to expand the population of cyber professionals and reconsider biases in algorithms and technology, the impact of these recent interventions has been marginal.

In 2021, only half of the schools in the US offer a substantial stand-alone course in computer science in high school. Students with the least access to computer science courses are African Americans, Hispanics, Native Americans, and students from rural areas (*K12 Computer Science Framework*, 2016b). The COVID-19 pandemic and the Black Lives Matter movement are exposing systemic structures of racism in America, including the severe inequities in access to cyber education. In addition, the pandemic has further exposed the effects of the digital divide, ready access to the Internet, and appropriate productivity tools, such as a laptop or home computer. This technology gap further hinders STEM and cyber ethics education in underserved populations. An infusion of ethics into cyber dialogs and policy debates is pertinent to be able to foster ethical dialogs and create equity and inclusion in cyber education.

Complexity of Environments across Businesses & Institutions in the US

Our world today is a data-driven, technology-enabled, hyper-connected ecosystem connected by the Internet of Things (IoT). We have combined our personal and professional environments with every technology possible to make things more connected, convenient, and interoperable. We benefit from the reach of the Internet, the volume of collected big data, and the sheer power of emerging technologies, if accessible. As a result, we have also created not only a dependency on technology, but incredible vulnerabilities to these ecosystems. Greengard reinforces this issue in his 2019 article, "What makes the IoT so powerful—and so dangerous— is the fact that devices and data now interconnect across vast ecosystems of sensors, chips, devices, machines, and software. This makes it possible to control and manipulate systems in ways that were never intended" (Greengard,

2019). As the rapid pace of technology and threats has expanded, leaders across sectors remain underprepared and under-educated in what is needed to combat cyber threats and inequities. Cyber ethics knowledge remains in isolated silos of IT specialists and cyber security professions, leaving leaders across sectors and citizens at large underprepared to confront cyber threats.

Our current environment during the COVID-19 pandemic consists of a very large percentage of the workforce working remotely from home in makeshift offices on personal networks. Teachers are conducting online and remote instruction for the first time using many tools with little to no training. The Boston Consulting Group (BCG) conducted a study in March 2020 on remote work with a focus on cyber security. They estimated about "30 million people are working from home in the US and over 300 million worldwide," using varying technologies including personal mobile phone and computers. Without good training and security protocols, many of these remote workers may fall victim to social engineering, phishing schemes, and cyberattacks, as Coden Et al cautions, "Cyberattacks are like the COVID-19 virus itself. Patching your systems is like washing your hands. And not clicking on phishing emails is like not touching your face," (Coden, et al, 2020).

Systemic Injustice and Constricted Leadership in Cyber Ethics Education

The roots of cyber ethics leadership deficits circulate back to a faulty pipeline of cyber ethics education and pervasive inequities in access to computer science education. Following World War II, computer science rapidly accelerated, yet only a select group of professionals and leaders participated in the creation of this new industry (Curtis, 2012; O'Regan, 2016; Reilly, 2003). As computer science graduate degree programs expanded in the 1970s and 1980s, the students enrolling in these courses remained comprised predominately of white males from middle to high-income backgrounds. These select computer scientists, as well as a small group of philosophers and science fiction writers, were among the first to consider the ethical ramifications of computer science technology. For example, Isaac Asimov's three laws of robotics continues to influence cyberlaw and ethics (Asimov, 1950). The application of ethics to the field of computer science also began to be debated among policy experts (Curtis, 2012). Yet, in the early years of the computer age, morals and ethics were primarily debated on the periphery. Leadership placed greater attention to competitive advantage and technological innovation in the Cold War landscape over ethical and justice implications.

The birth of the personal computer (PC) created an expansion in computer science courses and a slight growth in ethical considerations and policies governing computer use. From the onset, access to computers in American public schools was highly skewed to high-income districts, with low-income districts facing limited resources for computers (Kirby et al., 1990).

Throughout the 1990s, US computer science education expanded in K-12 schools. School districts began to (1) offer computer science courses across K-12, (2) build computer labs for all students to access, and (3) create specialized programs for gifted and talented students. While the numbers of computers per student increased as a result of additional Title I funds, schools faced a deficit in teachers with the skills to actually instruct computing. In 1996, only fifteen percent of teachers had received nine hours of instruction in educational technology (Parker & Davey, 2014). Through gifted and talented programs, some school districts acquired advanced computing technology, such as robotics and coding software, and could train small groups of students in advanced computing. Instructors of gifted and talented programs could receive specialized training or draw on university programs offering high school outreach. The extent to which cyber ethics was considered in these new educational programs is marginally covered in literature. Additionally, there is limited literature on the experience and outcomes of computer science education as a field because states did not have explicit computer science standards for K–12 until recently (Tilley-Coulson, 2016). Computer science content is often imbedded in math and science standards, making assessment challenging (Tatnall & Davey, 2014). In 2016, only five states had independent computer science standards and by 2019, thirty-four states had adopted computer science standards with mixed degrees of implementation (Education, 2019; Tilley-Coulson, 2016).

Even as access standardized computer science education grows, persistent inequities remain. As of 2015, only five percent of US high school students enroll in the AP Computer Science course and only fifty percent of students have access to a computer science course, with low-income school districts in rural and urban populations being disadvantaged (*K12 Computer Science Framework*, 2016b). Complicating the implementation of quality of computer science courses is the evidence that the majority of superintendents, principals, teachers, students, and parents are unable to differentiate between computer literacy (typing and being able to use basic computer functions) and computer science (Wang & Ravitz, 2016). In another survey, pre-service teachers were not prepared to model or teach cyber ethics, cyber security, and cyber safety due to limited knowledge of subjects and could only model four percent of the skills needed to instruct cyber ethics, cyber security, and cyber safety. The report illuminated the advanced skills required to ensure cyber security in the classroom. The effect of limited computer science education and inadequate cyber ethics training for students results in most students becoming passive users of technology and a marginal number of students become interactive critical users of computing technology or creators of cyber content. This lack of understanding about the mechanisms, function, and critical use of cyber technologies makes American citizens especially vulnerable to malicious cyber threats.

Shortfalls in Current Cyber Leadership: The Integrative Cyber Skills Model

Over the past decade, cyber leaders witnessed the exponential rise in digital technology spurred by the rapid adoption of smart devices. The precipitous change left leaders across industry and educational sectors at a loss on how to train workers and educate students on digital technology. Often students and junior colleagues demonstrated higher cyber competencies than their teachers and supervisors/leaders. With few models to draw on, a reactive leadership approach ensued, with leaders across sectors adopting an integrative cyber skills education strategy across industry and subjects with cyber skills being learned in relation to job-function or subject-function vs. a comprehensive competency approach. Examples of integrated cyber skills in the K-12 and higher education classroom include (1) online software to organize and deliver course content, (2) social media, (3) real time and recorded video, (4) instant access to film, music, speeches, and lectures, (5) digital course material, (6) instant access to digital data, and (7) ability to connect quickly with students via email and chat for course questions (Cambridge Assessment International Education, 2017). The rationale for the adoption of integrative cyber education has been due to (1) the rapid integration of technology into almost all disciplines and careers and (2) the limited availability of advanced computer science resources and teachers (Education, 2019; *K12 Computer Science Framework*, 2016b).

The integration of cyber into the curriculum has helped to facilitate a growth in (1) collaborative and social learning, (2) interdisciplinary learning, (3) accessible and adaptive learning. Additionally, researchers are beginning to notice positive effects on student learning in classes facilitated with digital technology compared to traditional classrooms including (1) positive influence on learning motivation, (2) increased intercultural and global knowledge, (3) an increase in interdisciplinary learning (Lin & Chen, 2017; Tiven & Fuchs, 2018). It should also be acknowledged that large-scale evaluation of the effects of digital and cyber education is an emerging field, and some studies have reported mixed results and negative learning outcomes including (1) a decrease in attention, (2) a decrease in writing and reading, (3) an increase in cyberbullying, and (4) an emphasis on quantitative content at the expense of the arts and the humanities (OECD, 2019; Rodideal, 2018; Taylor, 2012). More research is required to determine the effectiveness and outcomes of digital learning, particularly when the classroom moves to a fully online format as was the case during the global COVID-19 pandemic.

While the integrative approach has provided an immediate adoption of technology in the workplace and classroom, the critical and ethical use of technology has been marginally considered. There is wide consensus that an integrative computer science curriculum is not enough for the long-term needs of the future work force (Gross, 2018). In addition to integrating digital technologies, organizations and educators are advocating for the need to adopt computer science education, which includes cyber ethics more broadly as a discipline unto itself to support the advancement of graduates that can be creators of cyber content rather than only cyber users (*K12 Computer Science Framework*, 2016b). Additionally, there is a strong demand from educators to increase the research and assessment on cyber ethics education to determine most effective models and training (Oslejsek et al., 2020).

As advanced cyber education is often introduced only in specialized programs at the undergraduate and graduate level, professional training in cybersecurity and information technology has emerged as way to educate workers on the job on cyber technologies and protect against cyber threats. Additionally, tech firms, as well as the National Security Administration, certain government agencies, and the US Department of Defense offer their own comprehensive skills training to specifically address the cyber security needs of their organization's own workforce (US Cyber Command, 2020).

Reconsidering Cyber Ethics Paradigms

Over the past decade the field of cyber ethics has emerged alongside the expansion of the cybersecurity and the tech industry. Several news events have also pushed the topic of cyber ethics to the forefront of national attention including (1) the disclosure of the US drone warfare program (2) the Facebook–Cambridge Data Analytica scandal, (3) Russian interference in the US elections, (4) the misinformation campaigns populating Twitter and Facebook during the 2020 election and post-election period, among many more. Case analysis of these cyber events alongside emerging research into the ethics of cybersecurity, data and computer use, cyberlaw, and racial and social justice has promoted the emergence of new constructs and paradigms to investigate and evaluate cyber ethics. The events of 2020 laid bare the need to critically reexamine ethical values consideration in the cyber context. Enduring justice paradigms, such as truth, freedom of speech, and democratic leadership oaths have confronted uncharted cyber terrain that ultimately demand a need to reconsider what justice and ethics mean in the cyber domain.

The Constructing Alliance for Value-Driven Cyber Security recently published a report analyzing the ethical values being discussed in current cyber ethics research—see Table 2 for a summary of common ethical paradigms (Yaghmaei et al., 2020b). These data-driven ethical values demonstrate both the depth and significance of cyber ethics in cybersecurity and across industries as we enter the 2020s. While these values and ethical dilemmas are starting to be researched, marginal literature exists about the best practices for incorporating these ethical values and dilemmas into instruction and training for professionals and students (Yaghmaei et al., 2020b). Critically examining the ethical values considerations is pertinent, as the year of 2020 has left practitioners, researchers, and citizens with more questions than answers to cyber ethics dilemmas. An important initial aim is visualizing how these ethical paradigms might interact with values in the field of cyber ethics, especially in relation to the challenges described in the problem statement above. Specifically, how might PCD, rationalization of bad acts over cyber space, lack of individual and collective accountability, and a lack of cohesive policies governing data curation influence ethical paradigms and cyber values? (see Table 1 and Figure 2).

Table 1. Industry Most Common Ethical Paradigms (Yaghmaei et al., 2020b).

This table was adapted from the Yaghmaei er al.'s Constructing an Alliance for Value-Driven Cyber Security (CANVAS) Report (2020), with the authors developing the ethical value considerations for the education industry.

Industry	Ethical Value Considerations	Cyber Example
Health	Non–Maleficence/ Beneficence ↔ Safety	Do no harm online
	Privacy ↔ Security	Unauthorized access
	Trust ↔ Confidentiality	Patient health records
	Autonomy ↔ Consent	Decisions about their health data
	Equality ↔ Accessibility	Unequal treatment due to degree of digital literacy
	Fairness ↔ Justice	Hidden costs of technology
Business	Security Breaches ↔ Confidentiality	Lost data threat to privacy
	Security, Transparency, & Control	Third party data use
	Security, Compliance, Costs & Benefits	Does everyone follow data security?
	Access, Privacy, & Data Integrity	Hackers promoting free flow of information
	Security, Profit, & Data Accuracy	Offshore/ Outsource and data security concerns
	Consent & Trust	Surveillance
	Security, Acceptability, & Usability	Internet use code of conduct
National Security	Accessibility ↔ Security	Not trained to protect self/nation online
	Legality ↔ Safety/Security	Laws slow to respond to new technology
	Privacy/ Protection of Data ↔ Security	Individual vs. state security
	Confidentiality ↔ Trust	Fake Russian Facebook accounts spreading disinformation eroding public trust in news
	Connectedness ↔ Equity of Access	Consumer/ producer equity of access
	Accessibility ↔ Prosperity	Internet as public service
	Interconnectivity ↔ Security	Digital Blueprint of troops
	Cyber Awareness ↔ Security	Rapid technological change

Industry	Ethical Value Considerations	Cyber Example
Education	Autonomy ↔ Consent	Rights of child vs. legal guardian
	Interconnectivity ↔ Security	Recording videos vs. disclosing data of minors
	Equality ↔ Accessibility	Disparities in access to the Internet across socio-economic status
	Cyber Awareness ↔ Security	Rapid technology change and lack of teacher preparation
	Legality ↔ Safety/Security	Who is responsible for the child in a virtual classroom?
	Privacy/ Protection of Data ↔ Security	Third party providers of e-learning, i.e. Blackboard, Canvas, Google Classroom, etc.
		Need to relook definitions for Education records and Personally Identifiable Information (PII)
		For Example, currently video recordings of classes are not considered Education records or PII.

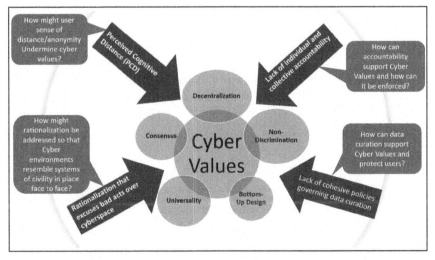

Figure 2. Cyber values and their challenges

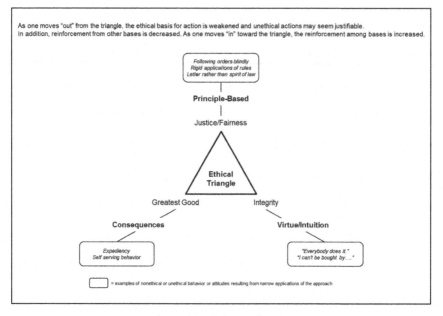

Figure 3. The Ethical Triangle (Svara, 2011)

Ethics Theory

There are three specific areas of ethics theory that could be useful in improving ethics in cyberspace. Those ethical theories include but are not limited to virtue, principles, and consequences (Pojman, L. & Fieser, J., 2006; McConnell & Westgate, 2019). For example, individuals motivated to do the right thing and live the good life might be impelled by virtue ethics to prevent unfair practices in cyberspace. Those who believe that the accepted practices and norms of the Internet along with laws governing its use would discourage cybercrime and cyber bullying may be using principle-based ethics. Finally, individuals who encourage the application of fair practices and equal access to the Internet because it is best for everyone involved might be using consequence-based ethics. Ultimately, to improve cyber ethics education, theorists and practitioners should engage in a discussion of combining all three of these approaches to ensure thoughtful and ethical practices and policies (See figure 3, Svara, 2011). Such a scholarly discussion would be greatly beneficial in the field of cyber where ethics education is a knowledge gap crying out to be filled.

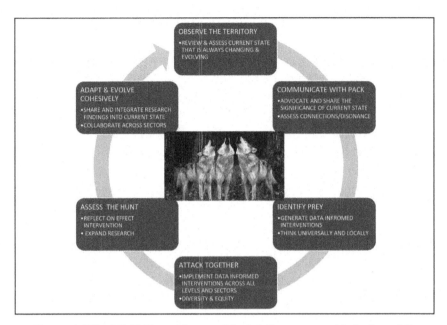

Figure 4. The Wolf-Trap Change Model. Image provided via public domain (Jooinn, 2020).

Creating & Implementing a National Cyber Ethics Leadership Change Model

In response to the current limitations in cyber ethics education in the US and the increasing pace and scale of cyber threats and attacks, a national cyber ethics leadership change model is urgently needed. Rather than a specific set of standards for different sectors and/or disciplines, the authors propose a broad-scale change model to be adopted and adapted across educational, business, and military institutions. This model draws structure from three change models: (1) Lewis's Unfreeze, Change, Refreeze model, (2) Kolb's learning cycle of concrete experience, reflective observation, abstract conceptualization, and active experimentation, and (3) Deming's change cycle of Act, Plan, Check, Do.

The six-step process described above in the Wolf-Trap Model has three core functions (1) to implement agile and adaptive cyber ethics education, (2) to promote universal cyber ethics education that is responsive to distinct needs of the industry or location, and (3) to build a research infrastructure to advance cyber ethics education and strengthen national security (See figure 3, Wolf-Trap Change Model). This model aims to create a national cyberethics leadership and education paradigm that is continuously adaptive to changing conditions, as the state of technological advancement in the cyber sector is constantly advancing. The model also emphasizes the importance of creating a template that is agile to local conditions yet interconnected as the threat from unethical cyber behavior can affect wide systems including public infrastructure, software, and apps used by millions of people. The model also prioritizes the need to assess, conduct research, and revaluate as the field of cyber ethics is emerging with limited resources currently available.

The first step of this model, "Observe the Territory," calls for the review of the current state of cyber ethics. This article is a first attempt at reviewing the state of data and cyber ethics broadly in the US, and this step calls for the development of additional reviews and observations across sectors and geographic contexts. Each wolf has a different perspective of the territory, and each of these viewpoints contributes to the development of a more accurate and cohesive strategy. An inclusive critical reflection of how we got to the point of wide-scale unethical behavior and systemic injustices in the cyber domain is a pertinent first aim for leadership striving to change and reform.

The second step of this model, "Communicate with the Pack," calls for the development of network infrastructure to develop and share information across sectors and disciplines. As cyber ethics is an emerging field, current information of cyber ethics is often trapped in disciplinary silos, which if shared can contribute informed interventions on a broad scale. This second step also identifies that there is public need to develop data and cyber ethics awareness for all citizens, as cyber behavior and threats have the potential to affect each of us, not just trained informational technology professionals. Cyber ethics is a national security consideration due to the scale of its impact on every user. The perspective of each wolf is useless to the pack if it is not communicated effectively.

The third step of this model, "Identify the Prey," focuses on the critical need to connect the style and scope of cyber ethics education interventions to the specific needs of the sector and current state. This step emphasizes the need to proactively design interventions to reduce unethical behavior. The prey is conceptualized as the gaps in our educational system that make us vulnerable to external and internal cyber threats. If we do not address and confront our own "prey" i.e., citizens needing wide-scale cyber ethics training, another predator will jump on our "prey" before we have any time to react. If we fail to intervene, our enemies force us into a reactive posture vs. proactive. Wolves who cannot identify the prey accurately and quickly may unexpectedly find themselves becoming the prey. There is also significant demand to frame racial and social injustice as an essential prey in the cyber ethics domain.

The fourth step of this model, "Attack Together," calls for the need to have data and cyber ethics educational interventions across all sectors and industries, including public institutions, for-profit companies, non-profit organizations, and the military. While each sector may have a different approach, each player—each wolf—should support the overarching mission to enhance cyber ethics education for all. Implementing interventions to reach all citizens across all socio-economic divisions is paramount. Diversity and inclusion are emphasized in this step, as systemic racism and sexism has created inequities in cyber education in the US that we still must challenge. Wolves instinctively know that for any attack to be successful, it must be coordinated, synchronized, and employ the appropriate number of wolves at the decisive point to trap the prey.

The fifth step of this model, "Assess the Hunt," draws from Kolb's learning model in which behavior transformation requires critical reflection, observation, and analysis. This step of the model also calls for the need to develop a research infrastructure specifically attuned to analyzing the effectiveness of cyber ethics educational interventions especially longitudinally, as the authors in-depth literature review found few studies reporting the empirical effects of cyber ethics education. Wolves must learn from their experience during the hunt and apply those lessons to future attempts to trap their prey.

The sixth step of the model "Adapt and Evolve Cohesively," emphasizes the interconnected nature of cyber threats and the need to share and integrate research findings across sectors. This step calls for developing networks, conferences, and policies that crosses sectors. There is pertinent need to strengthen and connect the needs of professional sectors with educational institutions to address the critical and timely needs of industry that is always changing and evolving. This step focuses on advancing national security by integrating and learning from the needs and research outcomes of professionals across sectors. This step brings home the foundational need of cyber ethics education to have a broad and universal mission that is informed from diverse perspectives. Wolves are more effective at countering threats when they stay in their packs, mass their power decisively, and adapt more effectively and quicker than their prey.

A Wolf-Trap Change Model Case Study

A short case study on applying the Wolf-Trap change model to improving cyber ethical behavior in virtual business school team projects, shows how the model builds critical, inclusive, and broad-change for business students on the topic of cyber ethics.

In the first step of the model, "Observe the Territory," the faculty of a business school course is asked to critically review how their current students are behaving in terms of cyber ethics. The faculty member starts the course off with an anonymous survey asking students to talk about their experience working on teams virtually and if they have encountered bad behavior, such as virtual lies, harassment, or discrimination. Students are also asked to comment on their own use of cyber technologies and social media and to identify challenges and dilemmas. By including the perspective of all students, the faculty member hopes to get a broader view of the problem-territory.

In the second step of this model, "Communicate with the Pack," the faculty member designs three learning assignments to broaden students perspectives and networks on cyber ethics, (1) the professor gives a pre-sentation and guided discussion on business cyber ethics and virtual teams introducing students broadly to the topic domain, (2) students participate in a group project where they learn about resources for building inclusive virtual teams, and (3) students are asked to interview a business leader who is working to promote cyber ethics in the workplace and share their findings with the course. By having students look broadly at the topic of cyber ethics, students will learn ways to communicate about the topic of cyber ethics across sectors and in the workplace. Students are also asked to develop inclusive virtual ground rules for their team project that will happen throughout the semester, to try to ensure that students are actively behaving ethically throughout the course as the course is delivered online.

In the third step of this model, "Identify the Prey," the faculty member has the entire class determine a broad cyber ethics problem statement that they want to work on throughout the semester, which they determine is the need to create inclusive cyber ethics programs. Each group then identifies a specific cyber ethics intervention to work on with their teams as their semester project. One group of students focuses on addressing the cyber disparities in a local low-income school. Another group works on examining the issue of discriminatory cyber harassment happening in their university. And a third group partners with a local organization to work on creating inclusive social media platforms to confront the challenges of the 2020 social media misinformation campaigns.

In the fourth step of this model, "Attack Together," the student teams work independently on a common problem statement throughout the semester but share their group project outcomes with the entire class in a final presentation and class-wide discussion. It is important that the student groups come back together to learn the ways other students were working on the cyber ethics challenge.

In the fifth step of this model, "Assess the Hunt," each student completes a reflective assignment on the outcomes of their group intervention and identifies strengths, weaknesses, opportunities, and threats to future work on cyber ethics. Students also share out their reflections in student groups to learn about the different perspective each student has on the project experience.

In the sixth step of the model "Adapt and Evolve Cohesively," the faculty member invites the student teams to participate in a school-wide virtual conference on cyber ethics where students share out their project outcomes and also learn from a broader university community about developments happening in cyber ethics. The virtual conference serves to teach students the value of continuous learning and adaption as a broad community of students and professionals.

The Leading Role Higher Education & Military Can Play in Implementing a Cyber Ethics Leadership Change Model

An interdisciplinary and inter-industry approach to cyber ethics leadership and education is required as the impact of cyber threats and cyberattacks is broadly impacting businesses, organizations, public sectors, and individual users. Both higher education institutions and the US military are in a unique position to serve as thought leaders in developing innovative and interdisciplinary cyber ethics education in the US. Universities maintain expertise broadly across information systems, computer science, business, law, public health, public policy, and education. The US military often has the most current and pertinent cyber technology and cyber security resources to protect our national security. The collaborative expertise of both higher education and the US military has the potential to deploy cyber ethics training to students and professionals broadly. This educational and ethics reflection process is especially pertinent today as the US military continues to investigate new uses of cyber platforms that could have far-reaching ethical ramifications. For example, over the last decade,

US military intelligence collectors have attempted to capture biometric data (fingerprints, iris scans, and facial scans) from eighty percent of the population of Afghanistan (Jacobsen, 2021; Talbott, 2021). Since it is a war zone, few have reflected on how to curate such data. Who uses, stores, and deletes such data? Since such technological applications have made their appearance in the US, perhaps it is time to determine how this data is captured, used, and stored as well as who controls the delete key. This is a clear example of how much of a struggle it can be to keep up with the ethical ramifications of cyber. This is a key example of runaway developments in cyber the ethical ramifications of which we are struggling to keep up.

A Call to Action & Recommendation

In 2021, the world has never been more virtually interconnected. This accelerated access to cyber has allowed businesses and institutions to adapt and continue to function in the face of an unprecedented global pandemic, requiring citizens to social distance and work and learn from home on a massive scale. While this seamless connectivity has been a blessing, it has also diguised a grim reality. The forced embrace of the remote environment along with the necessary complementary technologies has created a noticeable gap in the digital divide among poorer school districts and underserved populations, causing even greater cyber awareness risks. As a collective, we don't understand the cyber and data systems we use daily, nor their ethical consequences. Rather than maintain this status quo, this article calls attention and urgency to intervene through the development of increased education, research, and theory and model building on cyber and data ethics. The US is underprepared to ethically handle the pace and scale of our data and cyber use. Now is the time to heed Ian Malcolm's warning given in *Jurassic Park* about the risks of using an unknown technology that brings dinosaurs back to life without understanding the consequences of that technology. Now is the time to investigate, study, and train ourselves to be more critical and ethical cyber users before we experience an unintended consequence or cyberattack or cyber-instigated violence that leaves us incapable of rebooting.

Figure 5. Call to Action/Future Research Topics

References

Asimov, I. (1950). *I, Robot*. Spectra.

Benjamin, R. (2019). *Race After Technology*. Polity Press.

Berners-Lee, T., & Fischetti, M. (2000). Weaving the Web: The Orginial Design and Ultimate Destiny of the World Wide Web. Harper Business.

Brantly, A. F. (2016). The Most Governed Ungoverned Space: Legal and Policy Constraints on Military Operations in Cyberspace. *SAIS Review of International Affairs, 36*(2), 29–39. https://doi.org/10.1353

Cambridge Assessment International Education. (2017). Digital technologies in the classroom. Collaborate Ultra—File and Recording Storage FAQ. (2020, July 2). https://blackboard.secure.force.com/publickbarticleview?id=kA770000000CbqL

Craig, R. (2019, November). Closing the Cybersecurity skills gap. *Forbes2*.

Curtis, R. (2012). Computer Science Education Past and Radical Changes for Future. In T. Greening (Ed.), *Computer Science Education in the 21st Century* (19–27). Springer.

Education, C. S. (2019). *State of Computer Science Education Equity and Diversity*. Greening, T. (Ed.). (2012). *Computer Science Education in the 21st Century*. Springer.

Greenstein, S. (2020). The basic economics of Internet infrastructure. *Journal of Economic Perspectives, 34*(2), 192–214. https://doi.org/10.1257/jep.34.2.192.

Gross, A. (2018). Survey Large Gap Between Demand for Computer Science, Schools Actually Teaching It. 1–3.

Hlavac, G. C. Esq., & Easterly, E. J. Esq. (2015, April 1). *FERPA Primer: The Basics and Beyond*. National Association of Colleges and Employers (NACE). https://www.naceweb.org/public-policy-and-legal/legal-issues/ferpa-primer-the-basics-and-beyond/.

Jacobsen, A. (2021). First Platoon: A Story of Modern War in the Age of Identity Dominance (1st Edition). Dutton.

K12 Computer Science Framework. (2016a). https://doi.org/10.1017/CBO9781107415324.004

K12 Computer Science Framework. (2016b). https://doi.org/10.1017/CBO9781107415324.004.

Kirby, P., Oescher, J., Wilson, D., & Smith-Gratto, K. (1990). Computers In Schools: A New Source of Inequity. *Computers Education, 14*(6), 537–541.

Lee, T. (2019, November). How to close the tech skills gap. *Scientific America*.

Lin, M., & Chen, H. (2017). *A Study of the Effects of Digital Learning on Learning Motivation and Learning Outcome. 8223*(7), 3553–3564. https://doi.org/10.12973/eurasia.2017.00744a.

Lynch, H., Bartley, R., Metcalf, J., Petroni, M., Ahuja, A., & David, S. L. (2016). *Building digital trust: The role of data ethics in the digital age*. Causeit, Inc. https://www.causeit.org/data-ethics.

Martin, A., McAlear, F., & Scott, A. (2015). *Path not found Disparities in Access to. 1*(0), 1–16.

McConnell, R., & Westgate, E. (2019). What were you thinking: Discovering your moral philosophy using the forensic approach. *The International Journal of Ethical Leadership, 6* (Fall 2019), 60–78.

Mossberger, K., Tolbert, C. J., & McNeal, R. S. (2008). *Digital Citizenship: The Internet, Society, and Participation*. MIT Press.

O'Regan, G. (2016). Introduction to the History of Computing. Springer.

Oslejsek, R., Rusnak, V., Burska, K., Svabensky, V., Vykopal, J., & Cegan, J. (2020). Conceptual Model of Visual Analytics for Hands-on Cybersecurity Training. *IEE*. Transactions on Visualization and Computer Graphics, 2626(c), 1–1. https://doi.org/10.1109/tvcg.2020.2977336.

Parker, K., & Davey, B. (2014). Computers in Schools in the USA: A Social History. In A. Tatnall & B. Davey (Eds.), *Reflections on the History of Computers in Education* (pp. 203–211). Springer.

Petroni, M., Long, J., Tiell, S., Lynch, H., & David, S. L. (2016). *Data Ethics: Informed Consent and Data in Motion*. Causeit, Inc. https://www.causeit.org/data-ethics

Pojman, L. & Fieser, J. (2006). *Ethics: Discovering Right and Wrong* (7th ed.). Cengage Learning.

Reilly, E. D. (2003). Milestones in Computer Science and Information Technology. Greenwood Press.

Shepley, J. (2016, April 29). *Ignoring Orphaned Data is a Risky Business*. CMSWire.Com. https://www.cmswire.com/information-management/ignoring-orphaned-data-is-a-risky-business/.

Silfversten, E., Frinking, E., Ryan, N., & Favaro, M. (2019a). Cybersecurity: A State-of-the-art Review. In *RAND Europe*. http://hdl.handle.net/20.500.12832/2423

Silfversten, E., Frinking, E., Ryan, N., & Favaro, M. (2019b). Cybersecurity: A State-of-the-art Review. In *RAND Europe*. http://hdl.handle.net/20.500.12832/2423.

Spielberg, S. (1993). *Jurassic Park* [Drama/Adventure]. Universal Pictures.

Svara, J. (2011). Combating corruption, encouraging ethics: A practical guide to management ethics. Rowman and Littlefield Publishers Inc.

Talbott, C. (2021, February 11). 'First Platoon,' featuring a Washington state soldier, details U.S. military's troubling quest for 'identity dominance.' *The Seattle Times.* https://www.seattletimes.com/entertainment/books/first-platoon-featuring-a-washington-state-soldier-details-u-s-militarys-troubling-quest-for-identity-dominance/.

Tatnall, A., & Davey, B. (Eds.). (2014). Reflections on the History of Computers in Education. Springer.

Thomson, J. (2019, July 1). *Ethics In The Digital Age: Protect Others' Data As You Would Your Own.* Forbes. https://www.forbes.com/sites/jeffthomson/2019/07/01/ethics-in-the-digital-age-protect-others-data-as-you-would-your-own/.

Tilley-Coulson, E. (2016). National Association of State Boards of Education States Move toward Computer Science Standards. *National Association of State Boards of Education, 23*(17).

Tiven, B. M. B., & Fuchs, E. R. (2018). Evaluating Global Digital Education: Student Outcomes Framework.

Wang, J., & Ravitz, J. (2016). Landscape of K-12 Computer Science Education in the U. S.: Perceptions, Access, and Barriers. *SIGCSE '16: Proceedings of the 47th ACM Technical Symposium on Computing Science Education,* 645–650.

White, G., Ariyanchandra, T., & White, D. (2019). Big Data, Ethics, and Social Impact Theory – A Conceptual Framework. *The Journal of Management and Engineering Integration, 12*(1), 9–15.

Yaghmaei, E., Poel, I. van de, Christen, M., Gordjin, B., Kleine, N., Loi, M., Morgan, G., & Weber, K. (2020). *White Paper 1 Cybersecurity and Ethics* (Issue 700540).

Overcoming American Tribalism
Healing America through Common Purpose
A CWRU North Star Seminar and Conversation on Justice
February 16, 2021

Reuben E. Brigety II
seventeenth vice-chancellor and president of the University of
the South and former US ambassador to the African Union
Jonathan Adler
Johan Verheij Memorial Professor of Law at Case Western
Reserve University
Ben Vinson III
provost and executive vice president of Case Western Reserve
University and an accomplished historian of Latin America

BEN VINSON: At Case Western Reserve University, we are driven by
a vision that we call our North Star. It states that Case Western Reserve
University is a high impact research community. Where humanity, science,
and technology meet to create a just and thriving world. And to help us
further achieve that mission, we highlight diverse people, diverse opinions,
and diverse ideas, but always with the goal of engaging in a dialogue that
is civil and respectful. The series that you're engaging in today, the North
Star seminar series, is trying to do just that. We need conversations like
one that we're having today. We need to keep civil discourse and learning
alive at our institution and in our broader community, and we're happy that
all of you have joined us to listen, but also to participate, in the discussion
that will ensue.

Now today's talk will feature a robust conversation on how universities
can better lead during these fractured times and develop a stronger sense
of constructive civic habits. After I introduce you to our featured speaker
today, I'll invite our own Jonathan Adler, who is an expert in constitutional
law, to help me moderate today's discussion and later the Q and A session
with our audience. Now, before we move on, I have some people to thank.
I want to thank our partners on this event, and they include the Inamori
International Center for Ethics and Excellence, right here at Case Western
Reserve University, as well as the Cuyahoga County Public Library. We're

very happy to have you as a partner, and we absolutely couldn't do this event without you. We're also gratefully and incredibly happy that you're supporting not only this event, but our partnership in trying to work with our surrounding community for a better Cleveland and a better Northeast Ohio. I also want to thank as well and mention the Academy of Arts and Sciences who recently had a Commission on Our Common Purpose— that's the title of the commission—really to help promote a healthier civic dialogue in the United States. Their report was actually inspirational for the formation of this North Star seminar series. Now, without further ado, it is my pleasure today to introduce today's featured speaker.

Rueben Brigety II Is the seventeenth vice chancellor and president of the University of the South. Now he is bringing inspirational leadership to this institution that's also known as Sewanee. And this institution, actually, for those of you who don't know it, has a reputation for producing Rhodes Scholars, Watson Fellows, Fulbrighters, and has a partnership with Yale University itself. It's a jewel of an educational institution in the south, but it's also a place that has been deep in the conversation of reckoning with its own past as have many institutions of higher education in this moment. Now before becoming vice chancellor and president of the University of the South, he served as dean of the Elliott School of International Affairs at the George Washington University. Prior to that he served as a US ambassador to the African Union, where he served for two years. Now in that role he managed the strategic partnership between the United States and the African Union, with an emphasis on democracy and governance, economic growth, and development. He also served as the permanent representative of the United States to the United Nations Economic Commission for Africa, and earlier as Deputy Assistant Secretary of State, and the Bureau of African Affairs. Prior to his work in the policy arena, he was an assistant professor of government and politics at the George Mason University and before that he taught international relations at the School of International Service at American University. Before entering academia, he conducted research missions in Afghanistan and Iraq with the arms division of the Human Rights Watch. A native of Jacksonville, Florida, he is a distinguished midshipman graduate of the US Naval Academy and holds a master's degree in philosophy, as well as a PhD in international relations from the University of Cambridge. Without further ado, I'm pleased to welcome my friend, my colleague Rueben Brigety.

REUBEN BRIGETY: Well Dean Vincent, it's an honor to be with you, and I'm pleased to say, in front of all who are gathered that as far as I'm concerned, you're amongst the best leaders in American higher education today. I'll say that for free. You don't have to send me a check. Because it's true. I'm also delighted to see on the Zoom call my old dear friend of long standing, Dr. Shannon French, who is the director of the Inamori Center for Ethics at Case Western, and Professor Adler, it's an honor to be here with you as well.

So, ladies and gentlemen, thank you for having me I can just say just a few words to start and then I look forward to robust question and answer session. So as the Provost Vinson, I called you dean, didn't I? My bad, I'm sorry. I'm back to our old starts guys. As Provost Vinson mentioned, this is a time for talking in America. It has to be. I'm very heartened to hear of the philosophy behind the North Star speaker series. It is similar to the one that we have here at Sewanee, the University of the South. Sewanee was founded by churchmen, and they were all men at time, by the Episcopal church and our founding philosophy, our motto, is the first verse of the hundred and thirty-third psalm which in Latin says: *Ecce quam bonum et quam iucundum habitare fratres in unum!*, which we call EQB for short, and translated, means behold, how good and pleasing it is when kindred dwell together in unity. In the philosophy, underlying that song, is that, notwithstanding our various differences indeed behold, how good and pleasing it is when we find a way, that notwithstanding our differences, to do all together. In our country, right now is that a moment of profound fracture. We are at, one might argue, the apotheosis of decades of political warfare that have caused members of opposite political parties to see each other as adversaries more than as fellow citizens. The nature of the coronavirus pandemic and the politicization of its response have seemed to only heighten those tensions. And for a variety of reasons, we also find ourselves at a moment of profound reckoning on matters of race, the likes of which we have not seen in at least a generation. I have spoken and written about many of these things for years and, if you allow me a shameless plug, in the latest edition of *Foreign Affairs* magazine, which literally just came out yesterday, I have an article that is titled "The Fractured Power: How to Overcome Tribalism." And it draws on years of experience and how the United States is engaged with other countries around the world that have been riven by a sectarian conflict and seeks to draw lessons from those diplomatic experiences that we may apply to ourselves, not only as a means of trying to heal our own divisions, but also crucially, from my perspective as a foreign affairs expert, as a means of strengthening American soft power so that we may have the moral example of managing our multi-ethnic democracy in a way that bolsters our moral credibility and addressing these challenges elsewhere in the world.

As Provost Vincent said, I am the vice chancellor and president of the University of the South which was founded initially in 1858. Not only to be a center of learning here in the antebellum south, but also as our own historical archival research suggested, is the only university in the United States that was created specifically for the purposes of advancing the interests and superiority of the slave-holding culture and the ideology of white supremacy underlying it. Then the Civil War happened, then everything went up in smoke, and then the university was re-founded in 1868 here on the mountaintop in Sewanee, Tennessee. And for the first century of our existence, in addition to being in place of learning that, as Provost Vinson mentioned, distinguished itself not only through the number of per capita Rhodes Scholars we have, and so many other people that have gone on to distinguished fields and all manner of endeavor. Sewanee was also, self-consciously, a child of the old confederacy and a keeper of the flame of a lost cause for a century, only graduating its first singular African American graduate in 1970—a year after Neil Armstrong landed on the moon. Now, since then, guided by the Episcopal roots that anchor this institution, our university has made enormous strides, not only in reckoning with its past, but also providing a way to a future.

When I was named, elected as the seventeenth vice chancellor, almost a year ago now on February 28, 2020, the very last day of Black History month, that was just two weeks before coronavirus pandemic exploded. So, in that two-week interregnum, I was obviously, as any new university president was thinking about, thinking about how to advance the future of the university, enrollment, and financing a curriculum, and all those sorts of things, and hope to not talk about the whole race thing for a while, maybe they just wouldn't notice I was Black for a little bit. So you get to know me a little while before we can start to have those sort of more challenging conversations. And then the coronavirus pandemic happened. We had to evacuate our university, and, like every other higher education leader, I had to walk in the door trying to figure out how we were going to conduct our educational mission in the midst of a global pandemic of biblical proportions the likes of which we hadn't seen in a century.

And then on May 31 Minneapolis police officer Derek Chauvin kneeled on the neck of George Floyd in the middle of daylight, with his knee and his full body weight for eight minutes and forty-six seconds. Such that this grown man was crying for his dead mama as the life was squeezed out of him. And when the video of that was distributed, the world exploded with protest from Reykjavik to Rochester from Wellington to Washington, the likes of which the world had never seen, in spontaneous outrage across the globe on a single issue, and this issue was demanding that everybody treated be with basic humanity regardless of their race. And that was also the context within which I started my presidency. The first African American [president] of the University of the South walking into a global pandemic and the most profound racial reckoning that we had seen since 1968. It's a thing, and it's been a challenge. And I would say that, amongst the things that I've been most heartened by, has been the willingness of this university and this community to stand up and face those challenges, culminating on the racial bit with our Board of Regents on September 8 issuing a bold statement declaring categorically that we fundamentally repudiate our past veneration of the confederacy in the ideology of white supremacy underlaying it and, crucially, directing us to become a center for truth and reconciliation on matters of race in the American south and to be a model for diversity, equity, and inclusion in America. That's our charge. And so we're in the beginning of the process of figuring out how we continue to do that. And, just like you are guided by your North Star, we will be guided by our guiding principle of EQB to figure out how we can have these challenging conversations and still dwell together in unity. So thank you for the opportunity to make a few opening remarks, and I look forward to the conversation.

VINSON: Reuben, that is a penetrating beginning. I think you're certainly getting a lot of questions that are starting to brew in our audience. Before we get to their questions, we wanted to have a chance to have a little bit further dialogue with you, to get to know you even a little bit better. And to help me with that process, I have invited my esteemed colleague, Jonathan Adler. Professor Adler is the inaugural Johan Verheij Memorial professor of law and director of the Coleman P. Burke Center for Environmental Law here at Case Western Reserve University School of Law, and he teaches courses in environmental, administrative, and constitutional law. Professor Adler is the author of—or editor of—at least seven books and has testified before Congress numerous times and has been actually identified, in 2016, as the most cited legal academic and administrative and environmental law under the age of fifty. He has most recently been cited in the newly released US House impeachment report. Among other things, he is a regular commentator on numerous radio and TV programs, including PBS, NPR, Fox, and as I've recently shared with him some insights, even on *Entertainment Tonight* and those of you in our Case Western Reserve community are going to have to get to know that that story a little bit more. But Professor Adler, welcome. Before we get into a series of about six questions that we're going to pose to you, Rueben, designed to get to know you even a little bit better to get our audience to understand some of the issues from a deeper perspective before opening it up to them, I would like Professor Adler, if you wouldn't mind, just saying a couple of words.

JONATHAN ADLER: Well, thank you Ben, it's really a privilege and an honor to be part of this conversation, and it's fabulous to have Dr. Brigety here, if only virtually, in Cleveland. In the future we'll have to host you in person, when we can do that. But to be part of this conversation on issues that really matter so much for our country, for our communities, and as I think we're going to explore a little bit, for universities. Because I'm certainly among those that think that universities have a distinct role to play in figuring out how to deal with some of the tribal conflicts that our country is embroiled in and how we come through these conflicts in a better place, so I don't really want to take much time at this point. I just did want to reiterate that you know how much of an honor it is to be part of this conversation, how pleased we are that that Dr. Brigety with his range of experience, both his current experience at the University of the South, as well as his experience as a diplomat and in the State Department, as well as an academic and a member of the academy, the range of perspectives that brings to bear on these issues, and one of the things I look forward to particular to exploring, this notion which, I think, which started Dr. Brigety's article in *Foreign Affairs* poses and raises, which I think is important, but I think it's also challenging, which is thinking about the conflicts that the United States is wrestling with. A bit in the way that the United States has viewed conflicts in other countries, and given the history of American exceptionalism, given the way that we, the United States, tended to want to think of ourselves that's a provocative and challenging frame, and one that I look forward to our being able to explore in the conversation. But I'll stop there, because I really want to leave time for us to really engage with Dr. Brigety as much as we can.

VINSON: Well, thank you, Jonathan and I look forward to hearing what you've got to say and help us get a little bit deeper with Dr. Brigety. But President Brigety, every university leader brings their history, brings their experiences, and helps articulate and pivot and institution in a variety of ways, given that set of experiences that they bring to the table, you have some incredible assets. As a diplomat, as an ambassador to the African Union, What important lessons in healthy civic dialogue have you learned along the way? In your career path, especially in those areas where youth you've been in Africa you've been in the heart of so many struggles, how do you take from those experiences to improve civic dialogue in the university? What lessons do you draw from your path?

BRIGETY: Sure, it's a good question. So you read a bit about my biography and the various things I've done my peripatetic career. My father says, I can't seem to keep a job. And as its kind of turned out right, I mean, notwithstanding all these various things that I've had the opportunity to do, a kind of through line in it, for me, which I think this kind of as I approach firmly middle age, is a commitment to fundamental human dignity. Which is something that I think comes from my own background and upbringing in the South, in the southern Baptist tradition, as a student of the civil rights movement, as the son of all of my parents, aunties, uncles, whatever that fought that generation of the fight to expand the beloved community, from the words Martin Luther King. So I think that's sort of my entering argument frankly. I would also say . . . so going to the Naval Academy was my dream come true, I didn't apply anywhere else to college besides Annapolis. Shannon French can verify that I'm telling the truth.

SHANNON FRENCH: I do verify that.

BRIGETY: And the Naval Academy is a very special place and, notwithstanding all the other things that I've done, I mean, I think that it probably is still very much defines who I am. You can't wash that off. You're not supposed to, in fact. You know I hear when I'm making some of the decisions around here. I hear sometimes from folks, Brigety doesn't understand—it's not the Naval Academy. He can't just call it an airstrike on a fraternity house because he doesn't like how they didn't clean up their stuff, right? And like my view is I'm not calling an airstrike on anybody. But the one of the fundamental, foundational principles that I learned at Annapolis is accountability. You are, in every circumstance, accountable for yourself, accountable for your team, and accountable for how you expand your mission, and I would say to this point, accountable for how you engage and accountable for what you say. Because words matter, and they have power. And I think inculcating that sense of accountability in our discussion is very important. You know, one of the things I say to people around here all the time is you will never hear me use the phrase college kids. These are not college kids they are college adults, young adults, absolutely, inexperienced, yes, foolish, occasionally, but adults nonetheless. And as adults, you are always, in every circumstance, accountable for your actions. And that's a lesson that has to be reinforced. The third thing I would say, the skill that I learned in various parts of my practice, but diplomatic and otherwise, is the importance of proactively seeking human connection.

No matter what your differences, you can find something in common with anybody. You might have to try harder, but you can. And I have done that sitting on the ground, eating Afghan flatbread with people in the northern parts of Afghanistan. I have done it with local tribesmen in Iraq. I have done it across negotiating tables in Geneva. I've done it at refugee camps in Congo, and I have done it with southerners here on the mountain in Sewanee. And so in diplomatic practice, you say that trust is the coin of the realm, and you can't surge trust. You have to build it before you need it. And you begin to develop that just like you build a fire. I mean you find a tiny little spark, which is that essence of human connection because everybody's got a boss, everybody's got a mother-in-law, everybody's got kids that drive you crazy. You can find something on which to build commonality. You know this, to build a relationship and just build the foundation for creating mutual understanding.

VINSON: Thank you, thank you for that. I'm going to turn it over to Jonathan to see if there's a question you have.

ADLER: Yes, so I wanted to turn to the *Foreign Affairs* article which conveniently came out just in time for this program, which I recommend to folks, which talks about the conflicts that we're dealing with political and otherwise United States today as tribal conflicts and talks about the lessons that you've learned from your work as a diplomat and the like and how tribalism can be overcome. I was hoping you would walk us through a little bit of the argument of the article and, in particular, what we should be thinking and how we should be approaching these issues as citizens, as members of an academic community, to play our part in trying to reduce and overcome tribal conflict within the United States.

BRIGETY: Sure, well, I think, probably the most important thing to know about that article is I wrote it before the January 6 assault on the Capitol. And I also wrote it after a shorter piece that was published on foreignaffairs. com in October leading up to the presidential election which said that, as an American diplomat, if we saw any number of these sorts of things happening any other country—highly charged political environment, a highly armed society, media that is increasingly populated by hate speech dehumanizing the other, we would be ringing the diplomatic alarm bells at the highest levels of government. And, frankly, in advance of the January 6 riots, I wish I had been really, really wrong. But it only goes to serve to show the seriousness of our crisis of democratic governance, where we narrowly dodged a bullet.

And look, this is a separate question from whether you're republican or democrat. Separate question from you know what's your views on health care or taxation or anything else like that. Right, in fact, that's exactly the point, because the definition of tribalism is when people within a polity go to foundational identities and govern their politics on the basis of those identities, such that they trump, such that they are more salient, than overarching empirically identifying ideals and data. Such that those lines become impermeable even when the principles at stake or the evidence in question would otherwise lead a more reasonable person to find a possibility of a political compromise on a particular issue set. And so we have seen these sorts of foundational approaches to politics rip countries apart in Northern Ireland, in South Africa, in Timor Leste, in Iraq, postwar Iraq, in other places, in the Balkans, etc. And as you're the oldest constitutional democracy in the world, we not only like to think that that notion of tribalism doesn't apply to us, but quite frankly that because of the advancement of our democracy, we have lessons to teach other people. When, in fact, a series of empirical data suggests that our own political lodge are becoming so hardened as to essentially not simply resemble but to be defined by this notion of tribalism, right up to, and including, armed conflict.

The FBI noted in 2019 we have the highest rate of violent ethnic and religious-based hate crimes on record with the highest fatality rate, with the one exception being 1995 with the blowing up the Oklahoma City bombing, which was the Oklahoma City, which is such a particular event, but the trend line has gotten dramatically worse. We've seen the highest rates of firearm purchases in American history and the highest rates of firearm purchase amongst African Americans ever concerned about being subjected to racial violence. And so the data, I would argue, are compelling, in terms of laying out the danger in which our country finds itself, right now, which again it's not a partisan argument. In fact it's a fundamentally American argument for those who care deeply about the nature of our democratic experiment, which is not predestined to be eternal. It depends on what we do, which then leads to the second point to your question, professor, so what's the average person to do? So I lay out a series of things to consider. The first is the one lesson we know from every circumstance is that leadership matters. It matters immensely. And by leadership we mean the ability of people to reach beyond sectarian divisions, to face down not only their adversaries, but also, quite frankly, their allies who would otherwise prefer to be rooted and grounded in their tribal bastions for the purpose of building a stronger, multi-confessional, polity. Whether that be Gary Adams and David Trimble negotiating for the Good Friday Agreement or F. W. de Klerk and Nelson Mandela. Mandela, in particular, but de Klerk also gets credit as well, has to be said for making the hard political calculations that he needed to make in order to dismantle apartheid in South Africa 1994. Or Yasser Arafat and Yitzhak Rabin in 1993 and what seemed like the dawn of a potential final middle peace deal, which only sort of collapsed, for a variety of reasons. And so, and here's the thing, leaders respond to their people as much as they lead them, which means that as citizens, we ought to be demanding leaders that will find a way to cross the tribal lines of our society. Not to throw our individual principles away, not to have an imaginary kind of kumbaya version in which differences simply magically disappear, but they will find a way to help make our institutions work again, notwithstanding our differences. The beautiful thing about democracy is that people, elected officials are responsive to the ballot box. And we have to hold our folks accountable. It's especially true in an environment where our government is founded on the good side of the government, which leads to the second point. You also cannot underestimate the importance of civic society organizations on the ground. So as much as leaders in high political positions obviously have great import, so do those that are making individual connections and small individual communities. In church groups and in business associations and athletic groups that are finding ways to make connections with each other, so one of the things that Provost Vincent did not mention in his too-generous biography of me is that I'm an active volunteer at the Boy Scouts of America. I was a scout as a boy—I did not make Eagle Scout, which is a regret that I continue to live with to this day. One might argue the reason I'm an adult scout leader is to work out some of those demons for not making an Eagle Scout, but whatever right we'll save that for another day. But one of the one of the other reasons that I love, being an adult Scouter is that I find myself in constant connection with other adult leaders from walks of life that I otherwise not engage. Whose political views, whose religious backgrounds, whose economic circumstances are different from mine, and yet we actually find ourselves together around a core set of principles that are articulated within the scouting movement and with a core combined mission, which is to help educate and train these young people into being good citizens of tomorrow. And I would submit that there are lots of other ways for individuals to kind of find that, but yet, but we, but democracy is not a spectator sport, right, we have to get after it, get into it. And then there were a couple of other things that I mentioned, with the guards who, you know, structural aspects of our of our democracy that that I would argue, actually, essential that that helped to keep or improve tribal divisions, but I would say, those are the two most important things as citizens, that everybody on this call can do, demand that we have leaders that overcome tribal barriers and find ways in your own grassroots communities to break down those barriers on your own.

VINSON: President Brigety, very, very penetrating thoughts here. I think you are getting everyone excited about going out to get that article and read that article. Professor Adler and I are going to close with one question each and we're going to keep it somewhat simple before we open it up to the audience and hopefully have about fifteen minutes or so for their questions. Please audience, get your questions ready and we're going to set manage those over chat. So if you could begin to put your questions on chat. Jocelynn Clemings will help me, she's from my office, will help me manage those questions for me. I'm going to give you a quick one.

Even if you are a university president, you have seen dialogue work well and break down, you have theorized these things, What our universities to do? What is our role?

BRIGETY: I saw an article yesterday that was written in 2018 that quoted Admiral McRaven who was in command of the military operation that killed Osama bin Laden and then went on to command all US special operations forces and then after he retired was chancellor for the University of Texas system. So this man who's a career Navy Seal, toughest of the toughest Navy Seals, commanded all US Special Operations Forces across the entire military said that being a university president is the toughest job in America. Precisely in part, for precisely this sort of reason right, what do you do, I mean, how do you balance, particularly in a free society like ours, the notion of free speech to the maximum extent possible, while also drawing the boundaries of community?

Because, by definition, communities have boundaries. That's how you know if you're in them or you're out of them. We also, as places that are meant to be places of full free inquiry, also want to guard against creating a certain set of orthodoxies that prevent or preclude, falling truth wherever somebody may find that truth. All of which is made more complicated in environments, as we are today, where people can freely assert that some facts matter, and there are other alternative facts which also matter. If we can't agree on some kind of basic empirical truth, and that's hard. So I guess that that's a hard, that's a long way of saying that we have to be in the constantly evolving business of asserting what are the maximum broad values of a community that allows engagement, but also making clear that there are boundaries.

I will give you an example. So, regrettably, recently, here at the University of the South, notwithstanding all of the amazing things about our university, my family has been subjected to some harassment by unknown persons, doing disrespectful things repeatedly at our home, the president's residence, at night. Now, as these things continued, I bore them silently until for a variety of reasons, I felt that I could no longer do so. And so I gave a sermon in our Chapel, a speech in our Chapel here last Sunday, not this past Sunday, the Sunday before, basically saying these are tough times. I understand that a lot of people are upset about an awful lot of things, and many of them have made their concerns known to me some more respectful ways some and more visceral ways. But here is the line, back up off my family and our home. I forgive you, in the spirit of Christian charity, not even knowing who you are what the motivations were for why you're doing what you're doing. But we will not have this, and, crucially, we will be a place where everybody, regardless of station, whether they're the vice chancellor or they're not whatever station, maybe, where everybody, where we insist that everybody is treated with dignity and decency. We can disagree, we can disagree vehemently, but we have to engage each other in a way that advances our common bonds of kinship. Now, how a particular university community both asserts those boundaries while also allowing an encouraging freedom within them, this is obviously just like any other family would, like any other marriage would, this is a uniquely personal conversation, even as it as one that is common enough that we can understand it and see it, what makes certain families functional what makes others dysfunctional. And so that's what I would say what has to be done, and that it changes in every circumstance.

VINSON: Thank you, thank you for that. I'm going to pass it over to Jonathan for the final question from us, and then we're going to go straight to the audience and Jocelynn will manage that.

ADLER: I wanted to follow up on those remarks and maybe push a little bit. Certainly universities have a unique and distinct role to play as places where civic engagement can occur, where conversations across various differences can occur. Certainly today at universities, like the University of the South, like Case Western, people from a wide range of backgrounds and experiences are put together in a way that that might not have occurred before or after there at the university. And that creates unique opportunities both to provide a forum for civic engagement as well as to help train people how to engage with those who they think of as different and to engage with them as equals and as fellow citizens, as opposed to as the other. At the same time, universities are often under pressure, both internally and externally, to take a stand, to assert a position beyond the narrow concerns of what we traditionally think of as academic matters. I was wondering if you could say a little bit more about your view about how universities should balance those potentially competing considerations. And just lastly, one reason that comes to mind from your article is when the United States is dealing with tribal conflicts in other countries, we're the outsider, and so we can play the role of trying to encourage civic engagement without taking a side. But none of us are outsiders to the conflicts and divisions that occur within the United States, and so I'm just wondering how you see universities should balance that role, on the one hand, of being the place for civic engagement, but on the other hand, being institutions that will often feel compelled to align themselves with particular values or conceptions of justice that seem particularly important.

BRIGETY: That is such a hard question, it is such a very hard question. I've been in the job eight months, so I clearly don't have enough of a track record, but I will say this. I will say it from the perspective of both my current position and a previous one, when I was dean at the Elliott School. The first is that I believe that institutions have to have defined values. Here's the thing, let me say it differently, every institution has them, whether it has them assertively and self-consciously, or it simply has them by virtue of what it dodges or what it doesn't do, everybody has them. And so the right starting point is for every institution to sort of assert what its baseline values are and what it will tolerate and what it won't, which then helps you answer the secondary question, so if these are our values, how do you decide when to engage and when not to engage. Particularly as when you choose not to engage that is at least as much of a message on anything as when you choose to engage and knowing that everybody's always going to have a view. Sewanee, what I like to call the Sewanee-verse. All those people that know and love Sewanee, both our students here our alumni, whatever, Sewanee-verse is a very retail place where everybody's got a view on everything. It feels a prerogative to express them directly to vice chancellor, regularly. So the way in which I have approached this, thus far, and I'll give you some lessons of what I've learned, are, one, again we have begun and continue to be in the process of asserting and reasserting our values and leaning into those as a baseline of what our expectations are as sort of our conduct here. Second is, there are a billion things happening in the world on any given day that even if you assert those values suggests that you want to comment on them, right? And so the ways in which I try to distinguish that are what are those things that are directly tied to our values that are also clearly and incontrovertibly tied to our university.

Let me give you a recent example. So in the days following the assault, the seditious assault on the Capitol on January 6, and we started to learn a bit more about who these people were. It turns out amongst the very first group of people to be arrested and identified was a graduate of Sewanee, class of 1990. The man named Cleveland Meredith, it's all public information, so I'm not say anything that wasn't shared. He is accused of having publicly declared that he was going to put a bullet in Nancy Pelosi's noggin on national television. And he was arrested with a semi-automatic rifle and a pistol with 2,500 rounds of ammunition in a hotel room in Washington, DC. Now, when the riot first happened, we convened an emergency meeting here of the senior staff to ask, let's just kind of review our security procedures, and make sure that we're all good and should we say anything about the riot because the presiding Bishop of the Episcopal church, the most Reverend Michael Curry, did say something. We decided, no. Yes, we have our own values, but there is nothing that is particularly, directly related to Sewanee that we should say something about, so we didn't. And then, after about forty-eight hours, it became clear that this gentleman, Cleveland Meredith, was involved and, therefore, and that that information was being promulgated in the Sewanee-verse, so then we decided we had to make a statement. Issued what I thought was an incredibly reasonable statement, like everybody else and came under my signature, which is relevant, right?

One, like all Americans, I was shocked and saddened to see what happened on the Capitol steps. Two, we all have an obligation for civil discourse, as our presiding Bishop said. Democracy is a sacred trust has to be protected, and three, we know of as well, we know that there is a Sewanee graduate who's been implicated. We will follow the facts as they develop. Simple, reasonable, completely anodyne, in my view. And then I got a ton of email back saying why didn't you say anything during Black Lives Matter. Right? If this is really what you believe, why didn't you say anything when these Black Lives Matter and antifa protesters are burning down Portland and

Washington and whatever else. Now, fortunately, I could write back and did and say actually I did say those things. I said them on my very first speech on my very first day in office, and I said that again, later at the end of the summer during a sermon that I preach in Christchurch Cathedral about the importance of civil discourse, as we engage these issues and why I personally denounce political violence in any circumstance. There are folks who didn't want to hear that. All they wanted to be able to assert was that I cared and was prepared to denounce people that were storming the Capitol for whatever reasons they thought to be righteous, but I was letting these Black Lives Matter people off the hook. And so that's a long way of saying that you'll never get it right. And if you're never going to get it right, I have long since come to the view that I could declare that it is Tuesday on a Tuesday and have some non-trivial portion of the Sewanee-verse take issue with that assertion. And so you're going to take heat anyway, you may as well do so in a way that you can live with yourself with. And the way in which I think about this is, is it consistent with the values that were articulated, and is it directly relevant to our university, and everybody else can make their own judgments.

VINSON: President Brigety, we've gotten to that time. We do have a little bit of time for questions. I'm gonna allow Jocelynn to please manage that. And for those who would like to, I think if you're able to, President Brigety and Jonathan, if we can maybe have an extra five minutes, if possible, but Jocelynn.

JOCELYNN CLEMINGS: All right, Shannon we're going to start with you. You had your hand up earlier, I know you have a burning question, you can go ahead and unmute yourself as well.

FRENCH: Gotcha, thank you, I will try to be quick, though, because we have so little time, and I know there's lots of burning questions out there. And first Reuben, thank you again. So many helpful and genuinely helpful and inspirational and insightful comments here today, thank you for all of us, but I would also want to ask your thoughts. You've made it clear, and I agree with you, that we're trying to shape freedom within certain boundaries. But I do worry that there's so much language now being used by well-intentioned people about civic discourse and so forth, that we're actually not holding those boundaries hard enough, and we're not making enough of a point about how you do not need to engage with certain people. You do not need to have a conversation with, for example, someone who denies your fundamental rights. You know if someone is denying my rights, they're not just disagreeing with me. And I I've had this come up in so many interesting contexts, including, most recently, someone being very frustrated in the military. As a woman, being asked to again, defend publicly, that women belong in the military. And it was done in the name of civil discourse, so there's a sense I want, I wonder if you can comment on, because I know you've dealt with this of how do we defend people who shouldn't have to be the ones defending their own rights?

BRIGETY: You have just articulated my life, and, crucially, the lives of so many other Americans who've always had to be in the place where they had to defend their very worth. Let me give you two examples. In the last seven months, I've been in this job, my first month on the job I got a call from an alum, class of 1974. You know I told you, the Sewanee-versus is a retail thing. So that anybody can reach out and talk to the vice chancellor, I'm trying to make myself available and engage with folks. And this gentleman after exchanging pleasantries and talking about some curricular matters, he said, well Vice Chancellor, I just want to know that you're going to let all views be heard. I was like, well, what do you mean Coke versus Pepsi. I don't understand all views on what. And he said, you know, like about this like slavery stuff. You know, everybody knows the slavery was bad, but not all slaves were treated badly. Slavery was like the necessary evil to get our country started. I said well, it was evil, but it wasn't necessary. He said well you know, it was a business decision and in business, you have to make tough decisions.

I, verbatim, I'm telling you exactly what this man said, and Vice Chancellor, I expect you to allow all voices to be heard. So within my first month on the job, I am being checked, put in my place, attempted to be put in my place, by an alum who wants to make sure that I will allow the relative merits of slavery to be properly debated at the university under my watch. And I said, of course I would because I believe that the reason debate and checking it against the factually empirical record will do more to help people reach a conclusion than asserting without evidence what one way or the other might be. I'll give you another example. So after I told you about that statement that we sent out about the Capitol riots, and every person we sent back, I personally, or one of my people, usually me, saying, of course, we did, and I personally spoke out against you know file, type, and every circumstance. I got a letter back from one woman from Lexington who is being as charitable as I'm sure she knew how to be. Said thank you very much for that and, by the way, congratulations that they let you be the first Black vice chancellor of the University of South. They let me be, right? As if I'm saying ladies, congratulations that your husband let you be his wife. Right? And so, one more, one more, why not? I'll give you one more just for the heck of it so.

After my sermon that I gave sort of drawing the line of our boundaries, I got an email from another student. A young lady who's a junior who basically sort of was very apologetic and explaining how her mind had been changed as a result of my sermon and how so much hate speech have been normalized etc, etc. And to apologize, because, as the first Black vice chancellor, she was holding me up to a standard to be in this impossible, perfectly impossible great leader, and that was unfair of her to hold me to that standard. And I'm thinking to myself, I was a brigade commander in the United States Naval Academy. I have a doctorate from one of the oldest and most prestigious universities on campus in the world. I have faced down danger multiple times in multiple hostile environments all around the world. I'm a former United States ambassador, what is it that you think I have to prove to you? Now, let me say this for the record, Sewanee is an incredible place. It is a wonderful place filled with lots of wonderful people, and I would not be here if that were not the case, and I also believe in being honest in dialogue. So that we can all grow to a higher plane of understanding and our engagements with each other. It's a long way of saying, Shannon, that I guess I am probably even a bit more expansive in what I'm prepared to tolerate for the purpose of coming to mutual or better shared understanding, but even as I'm being prepared to tolerate a lot more, I find myself increasingly more and more firm on what the boundaries are.

FRENCH: You're a better person than I am, Reuben. And wow, thank you for those stories. Incredible.

CLEMINGS: Absolutely, thank you for sharing. Matthew, you're up next. You are muted Matthew.

MATTHEW KADISH: Thank you, thank you, sorry I had to find my find my mute button. Reuben, thank you so much for joining us. I'd like to throw a practical question on the table, and if you've had the chat on, which I think you did, because you were kind enough to send us the link, you've had a preview of it, which seems like fair play. I'll read it out for anybody that's not on the chat and, if it's too specific, or too incendiary, then that's fine. I thought I'd throw it out since other people are probably wondering. Since January 6 and the insurrection and given the proliferation of Qanon and mass radicalization in the US, how can we best defuse the tensions with and from the Trump supporters, and can we or should we?

BRIGETY: Sure, well first, with all due respect, I don't think we were acquainted with each other, so I'd be grateful if you call me doctor or vice chancellor.

KADISH: I apologize for that, sir.

BRIGETY: Ambassador or pick your title.

KADISH: Very good, all right good, correction taken, I apologize.

BRIGETY: Thank you. So look, yes, we have to find a way to engage our fellow citizens. We have got to find a way through this morass because the alternative is a low-grade insurgency. And, and I don't say that lightly. One might reasonably argue that we are already there with the levels of political violence that we are already seeing in this country. Now, I will be also equally honest that in the article, I did not write anything about the role that the media or disinformation plays in creating or tribalism, the reason I didn't because I don't have anything good to say about it. Right, I don't know the answer. I know it's a problem. I know other people have written about it, but I just don't know. I mean, particularly in a country where freedom of speech is amongst the first articulated freedoms on which our republic is based, I don't know how we simultaneously embrace and reinforce that freedom, but also say look it's got to be based on some facts. And, and let us at least try to figure out where the sort of Venn diagram is of a mutual understanding. What I would say is, that what occurs to me, is that a lot of people on both sides, on all sides, I think this is actually increasingly, so many people don't spend any time with any other people that don't think like they do. And it's in an environment like that, where quite frankly conspiracy theories are allowed to breathe. Let me just give you just one final example on this about why it's so important for each of us to engage and draw boundaries. Many of you may know who Dylan Roof is. Dylan Roof was the young man who in 2015 drove from a small town in South Carolina, not unlike, frankly, a lot of small towns that I'm around here right now, and drove to Charleston to the Mother Emanuel AME church to a prayer group on a Wednesday evening. Prayed with ten black parishioners, to include the minister, prayed with them for an hour, and then shot them one by one. Dead. Leaving one of them alive to tell the story. Dylan Roof was a neoconfederate bathed in the ideology of the confederacy and of Rhodesian South Africa. And he was a young man at the time he did it, so he probably was born, I think, in like 1998 or something like that so it's not like, he was you know from way back in whatever the darkest days of Jim Crow south. And so, his views were clearly known and clearly on display around people in his community. It does not appear that anybody called him on it. And so, this to me is an argument for engaging and remaining engaged with all of our fellow citizens to figure out how we can, just again, like that little sort of spark of fire that I told you about earlier, how we can rebuild some elements of trust and baseline understanding of our community to build and strengthen the center.

KADISH: And sir, if I, if I can circle back to the comment that you made before, which I actually wrote down because I thought it was so penetrating what we feel we need and may desperately want as a surge of trust, but we can't just do, that is what you're saying.

BRIGETY: That's correct.

VINSON: Well, I hate to break this up. Dr. Brigety, you could be here with us all evening and we could benefit from this conversation ritually many times over. This is precisely the North Star that we're looking for. It's precisely the North Star that's going to get us to a better tomorrow. It's precisely the North Star that our universities can embrace, to really help with the necessary uplift of our communities in our nation. I want to thank everyone for being here. I want to thank my colleague, Professor Jonathan Adler, for participating in today's event, I want to remind the audience that we have another conversation coming up just a week from today. And, who will be joining us? It will be the honorable Gil Cisneros, who is a philanthropist, a former US representative from California 39th Congressional district. He also has George Washington University ties. And interestingly, for those of you who play the lottery, his fortune came up through winning the Mega Millions jackpot, and his talk is entitled "Improving Civic Dialogue in America, a Congressman's Perspective" and will feature a conversation on the role of society, universities, private citizens, and our common purpose Thank you once again, President Brigety for gracing us with your presence and your knowledge. And thank you to our audience and hopefully we'll see you next time. Take care guys.

Contributors

Jonathan Adler is the Johan Verheij Memorial Professor of Law at Case Western Reserve University.

Reuben E. Brigety II is the seventeenth vice-chancellor and president of the University of the South and former US ambassador to the African Union.

LeVar Burton is the 2019 recipient of the Inamori Ethics Prize and a renowned actor and advocate for children's literacy and AIDS research.

Hans Cole is the Head of Environmental Campaigns, Grants, and Activism for Patagonia.

Stephanie Corbett is the Director of Energy and Sustainability and Interim Farm Director at Case Western Reserve University.

Gregory Eastwood is University Professor at the State University of New York and Professor of Bioethics and Humanities at the SUNY Upstate Medical University, Syracuse.

Shannon E. French is the Inamori Professor in Ethics, Director of the Inamori International Center for Ethics and Excellence and professor of philosophy and law at Case Western Reserve University.

Jacqueline Gillon is the Community Engagement Specialist & Diversity Coordinator, Thriving Communities for the Western Reserve Land Conservancy and Co-Leader of Black Environmental Leaders.

Ina Martin is the Operations Director, Materials for Opto/electronics Research and Education (MORE) Center at Case Western Reserve University.

Marian Wright Edelman is the 2017 recipient of the Inamori Ethics Prize and the founder and president of the Washington, DC-based Children's Defense Fund (CDF), which grew out of the Civil Right Movement.

Farouk El-Baz is the 2018 recipient of the Inamori Ethics Prize, a former Apollo Program NASA scientist and global resource conservationist.

Richard Albert McConnell is associate professor of tactics in the department of Army tactics at the US Army Command and General Staff College.

Jennifer Petrie-Wyman is assistant director and adjunct faculty at the David Berg Center for Ethics and Leadership in the Katz Graduate School of Business and College of Business Administration at the University of Pittsburgh.

Suzanne M. Rivera is the seventeenth president of Macalester College and a national expert in research ethics and science policy.

Anthony Rodi is a clinical associate professor of business administration and faculty director of the MS-MIS program in the Katz Graduate School of Business and College of Business Administration at the University of Pittsburgh.

David Suzuki is the 2012 recipient of the Inamori Ethics Prize, a legendary environmentalist, and a global leader on the issues of sustainable ecology and social justice.

Ben Vinson III is the provost and executive vice president of Case Western Reserve University and is an accomplished historian of Latin America.

David Whetham is the Director of the King's Centre for Military Ethics, and Reader in Military Ethics in the Defense Studies Department of King's College London, based at the Joint Service Command and Staff College at the UK Defense Academy.